2

16

40

OCTOBER 2024

COVER PHOTO BY ERNIE CARR

SCAN THE QR CODE FOR VIDEOS TO ENHANCE THIS ISSUE.

WDW
MAGAZINE

WDW Magazine (USPS 0002-2990), Issue 133 October 2024, is published monthly with 2 issues in March by CTSA LLC, c/o Freeport Press, 2127 Reiser Ave SE, New Philadelphia, OH 44663-3331. Periodicals postage paid at New Philadelphia, OH. POSTMASTER: Send address changes to Freeport Press, 2127 Reiser Ave SE, New Philadelphia, OH 44663-3331.

Hurry Baaaaaaack

Fresh Frights and Maritime Mysteries Expand Haunted Mansion's Lore and Legacy

By Brooke McDonald

After more than 50 years in operation at Walt Disney World, Haunted Mansion continues to exist in a delightfully unlivable state of unrest. You may have visited the Magic Kingdom's ghostly retreat 999 times, but keep your wits about you and look alive for these new and notable details. They not only pay homage to the Imagineers, past and present, who made the mansion what it is, but they also lend inspiration to the newest iteration of the Haunted Mansion, a nautical take headed for the high seas on the *Disney Treasure* this December.

WHERE TO FLASH YOUR GRIMMEST GRIN
It happens to even the most seasoned visitors to the Haunted Mansion: One look at your Disney PhotoPass ride photo reveals you still haven't figured out where the camera is. We've got you covered.

Welcome, foolish mortals. **PHOTO BY CLIFF WANG**

ABOVE: Keep your eyes peeled as you enter the Portrait Corridor for the lightning-flash transformations.
BELOW: Medusa's portrait hides a secret. **PHOTOS BY LAURIE SAPP**

It's almost too obvious once you know, but your portrait is taken in — you guessed it — the Portrait Corridor, which includes the load area and the beginning of the ride. Soon after your Doom Buggy departs on your tour, you'll pass windows to your left and portraits to your right. Dramatic flashes of lightning illuminate the portraits, transforming each subject's appearance from serene to spine-chilling — a knight on horseback turns skeletal, a lounging woman takes on the feline form of a Cat Lady (also referred to as a werecat).

While the Portrait Corridor concept and many of the portrait subjects date to the attraction's original concept art and designs by legendary Imagineer Marc Davis, the current effect is the result of an enhancement by Lanny

Smoot, an inventor with Walt Disney Imagineering who has more than 100 patents to his name. First implemented in 2005 at Disneyland and in 2007 at Walt Disney World, the updated technology enabled Imagineers to perfectly synchronize the transformations with the lightning flashes.

"The prior changing portraits required a roomful of equipment," Lanny told the *Los Angeles Times*. "It was a complex effect. My effect was so much smaller, and it gave the Mansion an instant change during the lightning. As soon as the lightning hits, the portraits change."

When your Doom Buggy reaches the last portrait along the corridor, the final lightning flash turns a woman's hair to snakes, revealing her as Medusa. Be brave and look her in the eyes; that last lightning flash doubles as the camera's, immortalizing your return gaze in digital "stone" as your Disney PhotoPass ride photo.

A NEW RESIDENT MATERIALIZES

If you haven't been to the Haunted Mansion since Nov. 30, 2023, on your next visit you'll find the furniture rearranged to make room for a notoriously elusive haunt: the Hatbox Ghost. The brainchild of Imagineer Yale Gracey, one of the lead designers of the original Disneyland attraction, the Hatbox Ghost illusion made the head of a hat-wearing, hatbox-toting ghost seemingly disappear and reappear, alternating between his body and the hatbox.

When Disneyland's Haunted Mansion first opened in 1969, the Hatbox Ghost was present in the attic near the bride. However, he only stuck around a week, quickly disappearing almost without a trace. So what happened?

According to the Disney+ series *Behind the Attraction*, the lighting in the space where Imagineers tested the effect differed from the lighting within the actual ride, rendering the illusion ineffective. A perfectionist, Yale insisted the ghost be removed from the ride.

Nearly 46 years and a lot of technological advancements later, another enterprising Imagineer, Daniel Joseph, took it upon himself to bring Yale Gracey's Hatbox Ghost back to death in Disneyland in May of 2015.

It took yet another eight-and-a-half years, but the Hatbox Ghost now haunts Walt Disney World's Mansion as well — albeit in a different, more controversial location. A master of displacement, the Hatbox Ghost appears in the Endless Hallway scene, where he has taken the place of one of the mansion's most famous pieces of furniture — an armchair (more on that next).

In addition to changing up the appearance of the well-known hallway scene, some critics take issue with the appearance of the Hatbox Ghost before Madame Leota's seance scene, long understood to be the point in the attraction when the mansion's spirits are first summoned.

WEIRD AND WATCHFUL EYES

If you always feel like somebody's watching you when you're inside Haunted Mansion, chances are Imagineer and Disney Legend Rolly Crump, one of the original ride's lead designers, had something to do with that.

Many of Rolly's ideas involved the personification of inanimate objects, such as the iconic purple wallpaper covered in watchful eyes and a chair that could stand and converse with guests.

The aforementioned armchair near the Endless Hallway, often unofficially referred to as the "Donald Duck chair" due to the resemblance of its visage to the famous fowl, was an evolution of that concept. Although Imagineers removed the hallway armchair to make way for the Hatbox Ghost, you can still spot a similar one in the library.

PREVIOUS & ABOVE: After decades, the Hatbox Ghost finally returned to Disneyland — and has now found a home at Walt Disney World as well. **PHOTOS BY JUDD HELMS**

LEFT: The so-called Donald Duck chair was an example of personifying inanimate objects in the mansion. **PHOTO BY JUDD HELMS** | *BELOW: Another great example is the haunting eyes on Haunted Mansion's infamous purple wallpaper.* **PHOTO BY CLIFF WANG**

CHARACTER MAGIC: EVIL QUEEN

BY TRISHA DAAB

Magic mirror on the wall, who has the best character meal of them all? The Evil Queen, of course.

The Evil Queen from *Snow White and the Seven Dwarfs* (also known as Grimhilde or, simply, The Queen) is one of four characters at Storybook Dining at Artist's Point with Snow White. While Snow White, Dopey, and Grumpy wander and dance around the room, guests must come to The Queen as she stands stoically in front of her mirror.

Villains really do have the most fun: The Evil Queen looks disdainfully as she poses for photos and elegantly signs her autograph, simply, "The Queen."

My favorite character meal moment, captured by a Disney PhotoPass photographer, was the sneer on The Queen's face when Dopey popped into the space and he and I both excitedly danced.

Need more Queen? Find her as the old peddler woman knocking on the dwarfs' cottage at the end of Seven Dwarfs Mine Train. Listen for her cackle. Or head to Disney's Hollywood Studios to catch a nightly showing of *Fantasmic!*, during which the Evil Queen tries to disrupt Mickey's dream. The Queen also makes an appearance at Mickey's Not-So-Scary Halloween Party. She's in the Boo-to-You Halloween Parade and has a cameo in the *Hocus Pocus Villain Spectacular*.

But if you want her to show you poses to terrify your stepdaughter or a few dwarfs, head to Storybook any time of the year!

Rolly Crump shows off concept art for Haunted Mansion to Walt and Julie Reihm Casaletto, Disneyland's first Ambassador. To the far left, you can see the Candle Man. ©**DISNEY**

A 'CANDLELIT' HOMAGE TO THE MAKER

Many of Rolly's oddities made Haunted Mansion what it is today, but so prolific were his designs that many didn't make it into the actual ride. Instead, Walt Disney suggested they be separately showcased as a Museum of the Weird collection alongside the main attraction. The Museum of the Weird itself never came to fruition, but the next time you ride Haunted Mansion, pay closer attention to just how "alive" with the sights, sounds, and movements of the undead the place really is — and think of Rolly.

Last year, a few months after 93-year-old Rolly passed away in March, a new nod to his Museum of the Weird appeared at both Disneyland and Walt Disney World. Yet another one of his wonderfully weird, iconic creations — a Candle Man, a flame-topped human-like candle figure seemingly molded out of dripping wax — turned up in the attic scenes at both locations.

You can now spot the Candle Man in the attic scene of Haunted Mansion.

A signature cocktail from the Haunted Mansion Parlor. **©DISNEY**

HAUNTED MANSION PARLOR SCARES AT SEA

Rolly's Museum of the Weird legacy, alongside more lore, is making its way further into regions beyond when Disney Cruise Line's newest ship, the *Disney Treasure*, sets sail later this year, bringing a new take on Haunted Mansion to the high seas in the Haunted Mansion Parlor. The new bar/lounge, which will occupy the same footprint as *Star Wars*: Hyperspace Lounge on the *Treasure*'s sister ship, the *Disney Wish*, takes iconic elements of Haunted Mansion and gives them a nautical twist that harkens back to the first-class parlors typical of classic cruise liners in the early 1900s.

In designing this space, Imagineers took inspiration from Haunted Mansion attractions around the world and from Rolly Crump's original Museum of the Weird sketches.

"You'll see a lot of nods to Rolly Crump and his amazing designs throughout the whole space," said Danny Handke, Senior Creative Director at Walt Disney Imagineering. From the tentacle-encircled marquee, to eyes lurking in the carpet and the classic purple wallpaper, to a version of the Donald Duck chair, "something's always staring at you," Handke said.

Not simply a space to sip spirits and zero-proof mocktails, the immersive lounge will also include a 30-minute story experience that will cycle throughout the afternoon and evening. "You're finally getting out of the Doom Buggy — you're getting to live in your own Haunted Mansion experience," said Nick Snyder, Walt Disney Imagineering Senior Concept Designer, noting that Haunted Mansion fans will finally get to turn the doorknob from the Corridor of Doors, touch the watchful wallpaper, and sit in the iconic armchair for a photo op.

The experience will parallel the classic story structure of Haunted Mansion, but will introduce a new maritime tale about a sea captain, the former owner of the parlor, who vanished after he was last seen on his way to the parlor for a special dinner with his enigmatic fiancé.

The Haunted Mansion Parlor's portrait gallery will further acquaint guests with some of the familiar and original spirits who now haunt the parlor, including The Mariner, created by Marc Davis, and new characters, the sea captain and his fiancé, whose transforming portrait puts a marine spin on Marc Davis' classic Cat Lady. The Mariner and the captain's bride will also lend their likenesses to souvenir ceramic mugs, modeled to look like they've been carved from a ship's wooden planks.

Upon entering the parlor, passengers become guests alongside ghosts at the captain's funeral. But, as on the attraction, the ghosts won't be able to materialize until Madame Leota leads a seance, transforming the eerie setting into a swinging wake.

Yet another homage to Rolly Crump's Museum of the Weird, the parlor will also realize Rolly's original concept for an aquarium with ghost fish. A purposeful piece of decor, the aquarium also holds a clue to the fate of the captain, whose hat was found floating in the tank after he vanished.

In addition to plenty of visual story nods to the original attraction, familiar tunes will be part of a custom musical arrangement by Shruti Kumar and Walt Disney Imagineering. Guests will also hear the iconic voice of the Ghost Host, the attraction's original narrator, Paul Frees, thanks to audio sourced from the Walt Disney Archives. 🖤

Want more fun and frightful Haunted Mansion stories? Get our Haunted Mansion Attraction Special for 32 pages dedicated to the mansion and its 999 happy haunts.

Concept art for the new Haunted Mansion Parlor. **©DISNEY**

SOMETHING WICKED THIS WAY COMES... TO MAGIC KINGDOM

By Timothy Moore

For years, Disney Villains have cowered in the darkest recesses of Walt Disney World, emerging from the swamps only to attempt to ensnare Mickey each night at *Fantasmic!* or to grab a drink in their lair at the Top of the World Lounge at Bay Lake Tower. If you want any closer interaction with these villains, you need to purchase a ticket to Mickey's Not-So-Scary Halloween Party (MNSSHP). Here, every villain from Hades and Maleficent to Captain Hook and Lady Tremaine takes to the stage to do the Sanderson Sisters' bidding and marches down Main Street, following the dim glow of the Headless Horseman's jack-o'-lantern.

But soon, Disney Villains will have a new place to call home, somewhere to scheme and scare without fear of Mickey's retaliation. Appropriately, their home will be called Villains Land, and it's coming to Magic Kingdom.

Disney Experiences Chairman Josh D'Amaro announced the new land earlier this year at D23: The Ultimate Disney Fan Event.

"Be prepared, you poor unfortunate souls," Josh said, referencing two iconic villains, Scar and Ursula, as he announced the new land. "It's going to be a fearless new vision for what a Disney experience can be."

We don't yet have an opening date for Villains Land, which means we're safe from their tyranny for now. Until they cast their shadow over the northwest corner of Magic Kingdom, Disney Villains sympathizers can count on MNSSHP for encounters with these evil rulers. 🖤

Stay up-to-date on the latest Disney news

Villains appear during the
Hocus Pocus Villain Spelltacular during
this year's Mickey's Not-So-Scary Halloween Party. **PHOTOS**
BY LAURIE SAPP | *Soon, Disney Villains will have a more*
permanent residence inside Magic Kingdom. **©DISNEY**

How To Celebrate Día de los Muertos at Disney Parks

BY JOSIE MAIDA

Día de los Muertos is a traditional Mexican holiday during which families and friends come together to celebrate and remember their loved ones who have passed on. The holiday, which begins Nov. 1 and ends Nov. 2, is the only time of year when spirits can return to the mortal world to visit their families and friends.

To properly welcome souls back to earth, families create altars, also known as ofrendas, dedicated to their departed loved ones. These ofrendas often include photos of the deceased, marigolds, candles, and the departed's favorite foods, drinks, and personal items.

Mexican culture has long been on display at Walt Disney World, particularly in the Mexico Pavilion at EPCOT. But since the release of *Coco* in 2017, Disney has found new ways to inject Mexican traditions, particularly Día de los Muertos, inside its parks, with special celebrations, snacks, and installations to commemorate the event.

Three mariachis performing at El Zocalo Park. **PHOTO BY DANNY SHUSTER**

Head to El Zocalo Park to see calacas and marigold flowers when the park celebrates Día de los Muertos. **PHOTOS BY DANNY SHUSTER**

DÍA DE LOS MUERTOS AT DISNEYLAND

While Día de los Muertos doesn't begin until the start of November, in-park celebrations at Disneyland begin in August alongside the launch of Halloween Time at the Disneyland Resort. In Frontierland at El Zocalo Park, located next to Rancho del Zocalo Restaurante, you can find larger-than-life skeleton sculptures — also known as calacas — representing a trio of mariachis. In addition to the calacas, you'll also encounter other traditional items, such as marigold flowers, or cempasúchil, traditionally found on ofrendas in Mexico and across the globe. In years past, guests have also been able to meet Miguel in this section of Disneyland.

After exploring El Zocalo Park, you can head into the neighboring Rancho del Zocalo Restaurante to continue celebrating the Day of the Dead. The restaurant, which serves Mexican-American food year-round, offers special dishes during the fall. This year, the menu features specialty sweet treats, including Churro Loops con Cajeta and Iced Mexican "Hot" Chocolate.

Across the Esplanade, Disney California Adventure hosts more Día de los Muertos celebrations on Pixar Pier. Here, you can see more of *Coco* come to life through decor and musical

PREVIOUS: The wooden Miguel puppet previously made appearances at EPCOT during select Mariachi Cobre performances. **PHOTO BY CLIFF WANG** | *RIGHT: La Catrina, now a symbol of Día de los Muertos, at El Zocalo Park.* **PHOTO BY DAVID QUINTANILLA**

performances. Perhaps most noteworthy, Plaza de la Familia, an immersive Mexican experience inside Disney California Adventure, includes *The Storytellers of Plaza de la Familia Celebrate The Musical World of Coco!* in the Paradise Gardens Park. The performance features traditional folklórico dancers, songs from the film, and puppets of Miguel and Dante in his alebrije form.

During Plaza de la Familia, you can also create your own paper alebrije masks, sample Mexican food, and experience what is perhaps the most impactful part of the celebration: the Memory Wall. Here, you and other guests can write notes to loved ones who have passed on and hang them from the Árbol de la Vida (Tree of Life) for all to see. It's a stunning collection of memories that connects us to the guests around us as we all honor those we love and miss each day.

Looking for more *Coco* to celebrate the Day of the Dead? Grab a ticket for the after-hours Oogie Boogie Bash. Here, you'll be able to see Ernesto de la Cruz in the... ~~flesh~~ *bones*!

Cars Land at Disney California Adventure also transforms for the fall holidays, including Día de los Muertos. Some of the cars get a fresh look, designed after traditional sugar skulls, an important piece of Mexican folk art used to celebrate Day of the Dead. In years past, Cars Land also featured an ofrenda erected for Doc Hudson, the beloved *Cars* character who played mentor to Lightning McQueen before passing away.

Throughout both Disneyland and Disney California Adventure, keep your eyes peeled for the papel picado. These small, colorful paper banners are a Mexican folk art tradition dating to the Aztecs, often depicting different intricate scenes. Disney does a great job of making sure each set tells a different story.

Ernesto de la Cruz performs during Oogie Boogie Bash. **PHOTO BY DAVID QUINTANILLA**

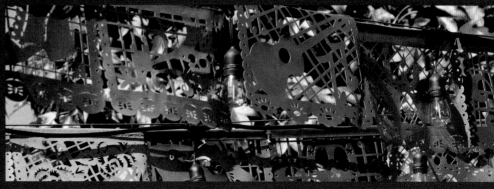

LEFT: No dead batteries here as Cars Land gets in on the festivities. | *ABOVE: Plaza de la Familia is a beautiful celebration in the fall at Disneyland.* **PHOTOS BY ABBY RICHARDSON**

Find a celebration of Mexican culture year-round in the Mexico Pavilion, under the glow of the looming pyramid. **PHOTO BY CLIFF WANG**

The pavilion abounds with Mexican folk art.
PHOTOS BY CLIFF WANG

DÍA DE LOS MUERTOS AT WALT DISNEY WORLD

At Walt Disney World, there is less of an official emphasis on Día de los Muertos, but there are still ways to celebrate the holiday in the parks, particularly at EPCOT's Mexico Pavilion.

A great way to start the celebrations at Walt Disney World is by listening to a set by Mariachi Cobre, the musical group that has performed in the Mexico Pavilion since opening day. The group plays mariachi classics — and once in a while, they throw in a song or two from *Coco*.

After listening to the musical stylings of Mariachi Cobre, you have plenty of options for Mexican-inspired food and fun. San Angel Inn Restaurante is a great spot for lunch or dinner to celebrate the holiday. The Table-Service spot serves Mexican-American favorites daily in the twilit ambience of the interior portion of the pavilion. Grab a table beneath the volcano and wave to Gran Fiesta Tour boats as they float past. You can also grab a quick bite at La Cantina de San Angel, a delicious marg at La Cava del Tequila, or a full meal on the water at La Hacienda de San Angel.

After filling up on traditional Mexican fare, learn more about Día de los Muertos inside the pavilion's Mexico Folk Art Gallery. 🐭

LET THE MUSIC TAKE YOU AWAY

Pin of the Month

NAME: D23-EXCLUSIVE *HALLOWEENTOWN* 25TH ANNIVERSARY PIN
EDITION SIZE: LIMITED EDITION 1500
YEAR RELEASED: 2023
ORIGINAL RETAIL PRICE: $17.99

This D23-exclusive Disney Channel Original Movie *Halloweentown* pin features the giant pumpkin statue found in the Town Square of the happy and cozy town that doubles as the film's name. For kids of the '90s, this is a welcome and nostalgic tribute to the whimsical charm of the movie and its sequels. This statue is a focal point in the films, symbolizing the heart of the town's spirited celebrations and magical allure, but the statue also plays an integral role in the movie's climax — don't worry, we won't spoil the ending for you. The pin reads "Halloweentown Est'd. Long Ago..." screen printed on its plaque, and the darker silver metal of the pin adds a spookier feel to the design. Here, Halloween is a year-round event, so enjoy your stay in Halloweentown!

Bringing COCO to Mickey's PhilharMagic

BY BRIAN MCCUMSEY

Orange petals of the cempasúchil (marigold) flower explode toward the audience as an orchestral version of "Un Poco Loco" fills the air. If it's been a while since you've experienced Mickey's PhilharMagic, this vibrant moment may catch you off guard. The addition of *Coco* to this classic Fantasyland show marked the first new scene for PhilharMagic in nearly 20 years.

The orange marigold is the perfect connection point to add *Coco* to the universe of PhilharMagic. In the festivities of Día de los Muertos, the fragrance of the flower is thought to guide the spirits back to the land of the living. Pixar animators used this idea to create an orange marigold bridge that connected the worlds in the 2017 film — and the marigold now bridges the world of classic Disney Animation and Pixar.

The *Coco* scene, introduced in the fall of 2021, marked the first collaboration between Walt Disney Imagineering, Disney Animation Studios, and Pixar on one project. Pixar handled the animation of Miguel and his world, and Disney handled Donald Duck. The combination of the two, despite the different studios, works quite well. At the heart of all of these stories is the desire for connection. The universes intersect in a beautiful way that seems natural, as if Donald was born to cross the marigold bridge.

MUSICAL MAGIC

Mickey's PhilharMagic is all about music, which made *Coco* perhaps the most fitting film to add to the attraction.

"*Coco* film directors Lee Unkrich and Adrian Molina were involved in the earliest brainstorms, and it was Lee who suggested we use 'Un Poco Loco' as the signature song for Mickey's PhilharMagic," said Roger Gould, Creative Director for Pixar Animation Studios.

When you experience "Un Poco Loco" during the attraction, you may notice some differences from the song in the film, however. Germaine Franco, one of the original composers for the score of *Coco*, returned to reorchestrate and rearrange the song specifically for the show, into what Roger called "the big celebration version of the music."

"In the original song, it was very small and kind of chamber music with the Mexican musicians," explained Germaine. "And this one, we added a full orchestra to make it a bigger sound and more orchestral to fit within the original songs that are in PhilharMagic already."

For Germaine, revisiting this music for PhilharMagic was like "going back home," she explained. "I always wanted my grandparents to hear it and say, 'That's Mexican music,' and feel that it was representative of our culture. And being able to do that through art and work is truly a wonderful opportunity."

NEVER FINISHED

Walt famously said Disneyland — and by extension all of his eventual parks — would "never be finished." Instead, they'd continue to grow and evolve for the next generation of guests. The update to Mickey's PhilharMagic to include Miguel, the film's music and stunning visuals, and the cultural traditions of Día de los Muertos is in keeping with Walt's grand vision.

"On the one hand, I hope that guests who see this sequence think it was there all along. We don't want it to stand out and be jarring, that suddenly it's not part of the DNA of Mickey's PhilharMagic," said Tom Fitzgerald, the Portfolio Creative Executive for Walt Disney Imagineering. "On the other hand, we do want them to know that there's something new — and that they get the idea that Mickey's PhilharMagic is a living, breathing show that can continue to evolve over time."

NEXT PAGE: Mickey's PhilharMagic's inclusion of a Coco scene marks a rare blending of Disney Animation and Pixar Studios.
PHOTO BY DOM TABON

THE MANY, MANY SKELETONS

OF WALT DISNEY WORLD

BY STEPHEN STOUT

E ach autumn, across these United States, Americans of all backgrounds purchase and display giant skeletons on their lawns. From Key West to Nome, they bedeck them in satiric costumes. Some buy multiples and make elaborate dioramas. Come early November, the bones are re-entombed in garages, attics, and crawl spaces or, in gestures of extreme laziness and/or defiance, left outdoors to weather the winter, spring, and summer months.

This ascendant tradition is wholesome; for skeletons, despite their sinister implications, are silly. They chatter in the cold and collapse into piles when struck in video games. All children know that a rib cage can be played like a xylophone. Dress them in a pair of sunglasses and a Tommy Bahama shirt and hilarity ensues. The use of fake human bone as decoration occurs across world cultures and spans centuries. Why would the Disney Parks be any different? Let us celebrate the scary, the friendly, and the *humerus* residents of Walt Disney World Resort.

ORIGINS
In late 19th-century Paris, three themed dining establishments centered on skeletons, ghosts, angels, demons, and the afterlife. Called "cabarets of death," their clientele were tourists, served drinks named "the juice of crushed maggots" (absinthe) by actors dressed like devils. Think: Tim Burton's Rainforest Cafe with The Adventurers Club whisked in. This fad was exported to American carnival grounds and is, in part, the reason there is a long history of dark rides featuring skeletons.

SNOW WHITE'S SCARY ADVENTURES
This opening-day Fantasyland attraction was notorious for scaring little ones. Adding to the litany of horrors were two skeletons located in The Evil Queen's dungeon. One had its hand outstretched, proffering a flagon. The other was manacled in the traditional dungeon prisoner fashion. The Evil Queen's crow, Raven, also stood perched on a skull.

INDIANA JONES AND THE KINGDOM OF THE (HUMAN) SKULL
Dr. Henry Walton "Indiana" Jones, Jr. has survived the first scene of his namesake Epic Stunt Spectacular! since the opening year of Disney's Hollywood Studios. Not so for the two poor souls whose final resting place is in what can safely be described as the only "murder trough" in the Disney Parks. Look, if you're going to enter a booby-trapped lost temple, you have to anticipate there being pits filled with spikes, lorded over by skeleton statues wielding heavy stone weaponry. It's the adventuring equivalent of knowing there will be traffic on World Drive after Happily Ever After.

TOP LEFT: Snow White's Adventures contained frightening skeletons, much like the version at Disneyland. **PHOTO BY STEPHANIE SHUSTER** | *TOP RIGHT: Similarly, a raven stood on a skull, much like at Disneyland.* **PHOTO BY NICK BARESE** | *BOTTOM: Skeletons also appear during the opening scene of Epic Stunt Spectacular!* **PHOTO BY CLIFF WANG**

MEXICO PAVILION

Some skeletons like to party — for instance, the band playing mariachi tunes on Gran Fiesta Tour Starring the Three Caballeros. These bare-bones animatronics are styled like calaveras — the Mexican folk art most commonly expressed via colorful, decorated sugar skulls. You can find multiple calaveras on display in the Mexico Folk Art Gallery's *Remember Me! La Celebración del Día de Muertos*, including the Everlasting Love statues and Mirror de los Muertos where, with a tap of your MagicBand, you can design a skeleton version of yourself.

A (COMPARATIVELY) BONE-DRY MANSION

I am shocked to relay that Haunted Mansion is *nearly* skeleton-less. Ezra, one of the Hitchhiking Ghosts, and the newly added Hatbox Ghost are gaunt, but do not qualify. That leaves the final slide in the foyer's changing portrait, The Ghost Host's dangling remains in the Stretching Room, the painting of The Black Prince revealing a skeleton of both horse and rider with each lightning flash, and the only real-deal pile of bones: a dog, or, more precisely, a hellhound tucked up on a hill in the swinging wake.

TOP: Skeletons in the Mexico Pavilion and aboard Gran Fiesta Tour. **PHOTOS BY CLIFF WANG** | *ABOVE: Surprisingly few skeletons appear on Haunted Mansion.* **PHOTO BY LAURIE SAPP**

SKELETON CREW

When Pirates of the Caribbean opened at Disneyland in 1967, fake skeleton technology was not yet capable of making bones realistic enough for Walt and his team. This meant the attraction was first populated with real human skeletons, which Imagineers later replaced, in all but a few rumored instances, by facsimiles, giving them a proper burial. To my knowledge, no human remains were used when Magic Kingdom's Pirates opened in 1973. The fake skeleton tech advances of the Nixon years, much like NASA, enjoyed a supercharged rate of progress.

These ex-pirates are meant to show the dangers of their lifestyle, yet their quaffing, sailing, and gambling promise an active afterlife should you enlist on The Wicked Wench. You'll find a firmer warning — the sign says "Pirates Ye Be Warned" — in A Pirate's Adventure ~ Tales of the Seven Seas, where several pirate skulls are on sticks. You should have anticipated such sights. When next you pass into Adventureland, look up toward the gateway's apex at the displayed skulls of some great beast and several ill-fortuned humans.

TOP: Skeletons appear in the queue and aboard Pirates of the Caribbean. **PHOTOS BY CLIFF WANG** | *CENTER: See skulls on spikes outside the attraction. BOTTOM: Also look for human and animal skeletons as you enter Adventureland.* **PHOTOS BY JUDD HELMS**

DINOSAUR(S)

Kids love dinosaurs, and Disney loves making "fossils." The perennially popular Tyrannosaurus Rex is thrice (and a half) represented in the parks. On Big Thunder Mountain Railroad, the great beast's skull has been given additional teeth to provide a more aggressive visual. Sue, the T. Rex in the courtyard of DINOSAUR, was cast from an actual skeleton at Chicago's Field Museum. A third tyrannosaur is housed in The Boneyard alongside pachycephalosaurus, parasaurolophus, mammoth skulls, and a traversable brachiosaurus. That half T. Rex? Imagineers wanted the carnotaurus fossil in the lobby of the Dino Institute to look even more fearsome, so they placed a carnotaurus skull atop the body of the larger dinosaur. Additional fossils are strewn throughout Dinoland and across the entryway to T-REX in Disney Springs.

TOP LEFT & CENTER: Dino skeletons at Disney Springs and Animal KIngdom. **PHOTOS BY JUDD HELMS** *TOP RIGHT, CENTER RIGHT, & BOTTOM: More dino skeletons across Animal Kingdom and Magic Kingdom.*

PHOTOS BY CLIFF WANG

A HYENA'S PLAYGROUND

Disney's Art of Animation Resort is dappled with climbable structures themed to *The Little Mermaid, Cars, Finding Nemo,* and *The Lion King.* After a dip in The Big Blue Pool, walk north, and you'll find yourself in The Elephant Graveyard — a playground built out of an enormous skull, tusks, and rib cage that is, to the best of my knowledge, the last skeleton used to theme an environment on Walt Disney World Property.

DANSE MACABRE

I hope we get more skeletons in Disney attractions, though I understand why Imagineers haven't been so femur-focused this last decade. A Disney day is spent in celebration, not contemplating mortality. But there's a pro-skeleton point to make...

Last Halloween, I showed a roomful of thirtysomethings Disney's *The Skeleton Dance* short (1929). While my declarations of "this was really impressive at the time" and "they sometimes make shirts with these guys on them" were met with polite nods, everyone laughed at the old jokes. The Walt Disney Company's use of skeletons for entertainment purposes pre-dates Goofy and Donald Duck. Skeletons are a company tradition; they are cool and fun and scary, just like the parks. I hope a long-rumored *Coco* attraction may someday end Imagineering's bone drought.

After all, it's a dying art.

BONE-RATTLING FUN WAITS FOR YOU ON YOUTUBE

TOP LEFT & TOP RIGHT: The Elephant Graveyard at Art of Animation. **PHOTOS BY MIKE BILLICK** | *CENTER: Shenzi at the play area.* **PHOTO BY RICH RAMOS** | *A still from* The Skeleton Dance. **©DISNEY**

Ballet Slippers, Buns, and a Bumblebee

Disney Character Costumes Through the Years

By Trisha Daab

A costume display at D23: The Ultimate Disney Fan Event in August. The display shows fabrics and costumes in various stages of completion.

PHOTOS BY DANNY SHUSTER

Vampire Mickey Mouse, poet Minnie Mouse, Darth Goofy, dinosaur Chip 'n' Dale, bumblebee Winnie the Pooh — these are but a few of the *hundreds* of different costumes our favorite Disney characters have worn at Disney Properties around the globe.

These characters have extensive wardrobes. Mickey alone has more than 100 outfits — scuba diver, space mouse, and George Washington, to name a few — according to *The Art of Disney Costuming* (2019).

The characters in their traditional garb. ©**DISNEY**

CLASSIC LOOKS

In the early days of Walt Disney World, Mickey, Minnie, Donald, and Goofy usually stuck with their traditional looks: a bowtie and red pants for Mickey, polka-dot dress for Minnie, orange shirt and yellow vest for Goofy, and blue shirt and, erm, no pants for Donald.

On special occasions or for photo shoots, these characters would break out different looks, such as a yellow dress, scuba suit, or an old-fashioned striped swimsuit for River Country.

THE WARDROBE EXPANDS

In the 1980s, Disney began expanding the classic characters' wardrobes. On the elegant staircase up to Monsieur Paul in EPCOT, Mickey once donned his chef whites with Chef Paul Bocuse. Minnie looked fancy in a feather boa while Mickey sported a tux for the opening of Disney-MGM Studios, now Disney's Hollywood Studios.

Mickey dons scuba gear for a dive at The Seas Pavilion.
PHOTO BY ERNIE CARR

Mickey and Minnie dressed as Star Wars characters. **©DISNEY**

One of the most epic looks for Mickey and his friends was during *Star Wars* Weekends at Hollywood Studios: Jedi Mickey, Princess Leia Minnie, Darth Goofy, Ewok Chip 'n' Dale, and stormtrooper Donald. For once, Donald wore pants!

Now, on any given day at Walt Disney World — between parades, meet-and-greets, and character dining — you can see Mickey and Minnie in at least 10 different outfits. They have looks themed to each meal and looks that are specific to each park, like Sorcerer Mickey and red-carpet-ready Minnie at Hollywood Studios.

Sorcerer Mickey at Disney's Hollywood Studios. **PHOTO BY CJ AYD**

WHAT ARE YOU GOING TO BE FOR HALLOWEEN, MICKEY?

Of course, there is one time of year when Imagineers really have fun playing with character costumes: Halloween.

How far in advance do you plan *your* Halloween costume? According to Walt Disney Imagineering, the process of picking and creating the character's Halloween costumes can take months. Imagineers always start by considering the character's personality. Then they go from sketching to considering color palettes, testing different fabrics, and sometimes considering how the costume might affect signing autographs.

I love seeing characters in costumes. It helps bring out another side to their personality. I saw painter Mickey and poet Minnie steal a kiss at Topolino's Terrace. Dinosaur Chip 'n' Dale at Disney's Animal Kingdom compared my braids to their horns. And there is nothing cuter than bumblebee Winnie the Pooh, pirate Tigger, and butterfly Piglet trying to make crying-on-the-outside clown Eeyore smile.

The chipmunks already dress as dinos at Animal Kingdom, but they get all the more more festive during the winter holidays. **PHOTO BY DANNY SHUSTER**

BEST OF CHARACTER COSTUMES

Best Halloween Costume the Character Would Totally Choose for Themselves: Pooh as a bumblebee at Mickey's Not-So-Scary Halloween Party at Magic Kingdom. What's extra cute is the costumes all look homemade, like there was a Hundred-Acre Wood "make-your-own-costume" contest.

Best Halloween Costume Poses: Elvis Stitch at Mickey's Not-So-Scary Halloween Party. With his pompadour, sparkly jumpsuit, and giant gold belt, Stitch is the *King* of the party.

Best Halloween Costumes Character Meal: Minnie's Halloween Dine at Hollywood & Vine at Disney's Hollywood Studios. You get to see Minnie, Mickey, Goofy, and Pluto dressed up and ready for trick-or-treating *without* needing to attend a party.

Best Character Meal Costumes With a Story: Breakfast à la Art at Topolino's Terrace. Painter Mickey, poet Minnie, sculptor Donald, and dancer Daisy have costumes so cute that you can purchase a stuffed animal of each one. During the meal, every character shows off their dance moves to themed music. Watching Donald enthusiastically clap for Daisy and then encourage the audience to do so as well is magical.

Best Holiday Costume: Chip 'n' Dale at Animal Kingdom. They're in their dinosaur costumes but with festive flair. Chip has a reindeer antler headband and Dale has holiday lights wrapped in his horns. ❦

Halloween on the High Seas
A Not-So-Scary Sail at Sea

By Brydie Huffman

My daughter stood, holding back tears and clutching her Jack Skellington doll. A concerned Cinderella knelt beside her.

"Mommy, I'm uncomfortable," Addie said.

I wasn't prepared to hear *that* on our magical family vacation. My daughter had spent 20 minutes picking out the perfect dress (she landed on the hand-me-down Rapunzel over the glittery Elsa she had begged for) and insisted on pairing it with light-up sneakers (in true 4-year-old fashion). The fact was lost on her that I had done even more prep work for this moment that she hadn't even seen, staying up until midnight to register for this Royal Gathering event on the *Disney Dream*.

I looked down at my princess and saw how uncomfortable she looked. Cue the mom-guilt.

I thought it would be perfect: a Halloween on the High Seas sailing for a Halloween-obsessed family. I had researched and studied all the activities we would do on the ship, including the menus for allergies, but I wasn't prepared for *this*. So how do you walk the fine line of creating Halloween fun for a sensitive soul in an over-the-top environment? It took some time to get our sea legs, but we worked it out in the end.

AUTUMN IN NEW YORK
In 2021, my husband and I put down a deposit for our first Disney Cruise. For the next two years, we saved at a comfortable pace to create the kind of vacation we wanted. To cut costs, we drove the seven hours to Manhattan (instead of a six-hour airport journey).

TOP LEFT: Brydie and her family set sail. **PHOTO COURTESY OF BRYDIE HUFFMAN** | *Halloween decor transforms the atrium on the* Disney Dream. **PHOTO BY KENNETH PALM**

The Dream *previously had sailings out of New York City.* **PHOTO BY BRYDIE HUFFMAN**

Driving through upstate New York in the fall is a magical experience in itself. Crisp autumn air and a view dotted with paint-by-number trees of red and orange set the tone for a Halloween weekend. We opted to stay in New Jersey the night before embarkation day, giving us time to explore the city in the morning before boarding the *Dream*.

The Manhattan Cruise Terminal sits in the heart of the action, nestled in Hell's Kitchen on Manhattan's West Side. We were nervous about where to unload and find bathrooms, but it was actually a breeze. Terminal staff came over and helped us with bag drop, which gave us time to walk over to the USS Intrepid Museum, a 1943 Aircraft Carrier at Pier 86. Through the winding drive and morning exploring the city, our daughter, about to embark on the first grand vacation of her life, showed no signs that she was apprehensive about the experiences awaiting us on the *Dream*.

SMOOTH SAILING AND ROUGH WATERS

Boarding the ship was the first time I saw Addie's joy levels drop. As we entered the stunning atrium, strung with festive garlands, Cast Members lined on either side, announcing each family as they came aboard. I looked back to capture the moment, only to see my daughter had her hands on her ears. We decided to explore the Oceaneer Club until our rooms were ready and get her more comfortable with the louder environments. The kid in me was drooling at this space: Crafts, interactive floors, and science labs were open for roaming.

With our daughter situated here, my husband and I ventured to the adults-only side of the ship and saw how the other half lived: quiet pools and hot coffee sipped in silence. From here, we watched the ship sail by the New York skyline and the Statue of Liberty.

But 18 minutes later, we received a notification through the Navigator App that our daughter wanted to be picked up. More tears greeted us at the door, and we scooped her up and went to the outdoor walking track to run out her big feelings. The same issue happened at the evening stage show; *Beauty and the Beast* ended early for us when she threw her hands over her ears and asked to go back to the room.

This was going to be a challenge.

CHILLIN' LIKE A VILLAIN

Checking the ship activities the next day, we made plans as a unit for quieter options. Craft time was the winner: an open sunny room with different DIY activities each day. I looked around and saw grandparents cutting paper masks for little hands, parents absorbed in coloring, and, most uniquely, no phones.

For nighttime (well, toddler-7 p.m.-nighttime) activities, we hit the silent disco hour — a genius concept. Each visitor wears a headset with three music station choices, which means the room itself is actually a place where you can hold a conversation since the tunes are pumping in light-up headsets only. Being able to dance in her own world without solo attention on herself allowed Addie to begin to blossom. It took some warming up, but here was the turning point for our daughter — and she was ready to enjoy all the magic the *Disney Dream* had in store, including the special Halloween celebrations.

I've been to some wild parties, but a Disney Cruise Line party is unlike anything else. From Pirate Night to Mickey's Mouse-querade to fireworks, we did it all. Addie still talks about the time she "danced with Minnie and Daisy" and went trick-or-treating on the "big boat." We learned to get to the events earlier than the listed time to allow her to run around and get more comfortable in a new space. We also enjoyed interacting with other families; the level of commitment to family costumes is unmatched on a Halloween cruise. My husband, a Disney newbie, asked me why so many people were dressed like spotted cows.

The Halloween sailing included a Pirate Night. **PHOTO BY KENNETH PALM**

He was pointing to a group wearing *One Hundred and One Dalmatians* costumes.

A pre-booked trip to Bibbidi Bobbidi Boutique for a princess makeover proved to be another quiet space my daughter loved — something to break up the go-go-go of a Halloween on the High Seas sailing. Brushing her glittery nails over the dress choices, she settled on the long-sleeved Anna costume (an odd choice on the day we docked in 80-plus-degree Bermuda weather). I'll never forget her genuine smile when they spun her around to reveal the final look.

CRUISING WITH INDIANA JONES

We hadn't planned to get off the ship, thinking we would use the time to explore the *Dream* when crowds were smaller and dig into the Halloween pastries. But as we pulled into the King's Wharf port in Bermuda, a historic military fort came into view. We learned it was a five-minute walk to the National Museum of Bermuda, and, having married an archaeologist, I knew it would be easier to go explore in person rather than listen to his historic facts about the island during another round of craft time.

Nestled under a cove where you can swim with dolphins, the museum's interactive kids' space was a big hit, offering another moment of serenity for our still sometimes overwhelmed daughter. While having a snack on the porch of the historic Commissioner's House, we could hear Disney music playing on the deck of the *Dream* at the bottom of the hill. Addie asked for a drink, then paused and added, "This is a good day, Mom."

A core family memory for all of us.

Craft time (above left) and Bibbidi Bobbidi Boutique (above right) were big hits. **PHOTOS BY BRYDIE HUFFMAN**

The museum was a hit with Brydie's family — and not far at all from the ship. **PHOTO BY BRYDIE HUFFMAN**

After our port adventure to the fort and museum proved this Disney Cruise held as much magic for the history-loving parents as it did for the Disney-loving kiddo, my husband and I decided to trade off solo time back on board so everyone still got the feel of a vacation. For him, that meant whiskey tasting. For me, it meant a guided tour of the ship's art — a great option if you can't get into Palo and Remy adult-only dining options, as you get to tour the spaces and ask questions. The former event coordinator in me had to ask about the Halloween decor during the tour, and a friendly Cast Member shared how Disney uses an external company to help transform the ship into a Halloween wonderland in a single morning. Each of the Halloween-decorated garlands is numbered on the back for that Disney-precision placement.

A DISNEY DREAM COME TRUE

As we disembarked on the last day, Addie introduced her Jack Skellington doll to his new road-trip buddy from Mickey's Mainsail: Ember from Disney•Pixar's *Elemental*. As she clutched both dolls, it was easy to see how much our daughter had grown from her first big travel experience — more confident and open to new experiences.

Our first Disney cruise, with its mix of *Hocus Pocus* magic and intimate spaces, had become a family canvas for creating unique moments where sensitivity and celebration were intertwined. 🐭

ABOVE: *Tina and her family at Minnie's Halloween Dine.*
PREVIOUS: *See the characters in their fun Halloween costumes during this character dining experience.*

Story by Tina Chiu | Photos by Jeff Chiu

Among all the seasons celebrated at Walt Disney World, Halloween holds a special place in my heart — admittedly odd, as I'm not particularly fond of being scared. But this is Disney, and they bring the family-friendly elements of the season to the forefront for younger kids (and us older scaredy cats). For years, I'd wanted to take my kids to Minnie's Halloween Dine, the specialty Halloween-themed dining experience with Minnie at Hollywood & Vine in Disney's Hollywood Studios. Here, you can meet Minnie and friends dressed in exclusive Halloween outfits. Last year, we finally snagged a reservation.

SPOOKTACULAR ATMOSPHERE

As my family stepped into Hollywood & Vine, we were transported to a wicked wonderland (Disney's Hollywood Studios is notably light on the Halloween decor elsewhere in the park). A large backdrop adorned with spooky decorations awaited us — the perfect spot for a quick photo, with the help of the Cast Member who led us into the restaurant. Minnie and her friends had transformed Hollywood & Vine with spooky signs and the latest Halloween merchandise. Our eyes darted from one spot to the next as we followed the Cast Member to our seats.

FRIGHTFULLY DELIGHTFUL FEAST

Minnie's Halloween Dine is served buffet-style, so we came with empty bellies to savor as much of the delicious food as we could. The buffet station spanned the entire length of the restaurant, with each side offering the same variety of options to ensure easier access for everyone.

KNOW BEFORE YOU GO

WHERE
Hollywood & Vine at Disney's Hollywood Studios at Echo Lake

WHEN
Check the Walt Disney World website for specific dates; Hollywood & Vine rotates between four seasonal dining offerings

MEALS
Lunch and dinner with Minnie are served buffet style; breakfast remains Disney Junior Play n' Dine year-round

PRICE
$63 per adult and $40 per child (3-9 years old); tax and gratuity not included

I especially loved how many plant-based choices the restaurant offered, including the flavorful Roasted Mushroom Farro Risotto and Crispy Tofu with Asian Glaze. Everyone in my family is a meat-eater, though, so we piled our plates with some mouthwatering proteins, including Salmon Miso Wasabi, Spice-rubbed Pork Loin, Oven-roasted Turkey Breast, and a special Baked Marinated Chicken dish crafted as part of Disney's Celebrate Soulfully. And, because it was the fall, Hollywood & Vine chefs prepared several specialty dishes with seasonal favorites such as butternut squash and creamed corn.

The lower kids' counter had plenty of options for picky eaters, such as mac and cheese, potato barrels, chicken nuggets, baked chicken, and corn dogs. My youngest filled up his plate with offerings from this section.

The buffet includes non-alcoholic drinks, though you can order a selection of alcoholic beverages for an additional cost. An allergen guide is also available to help with any food allergies.

Halloween decor and character interactions may be the initial draw of Minnie's Halloween Dine, but the food here is fantastic — and because it's a buffet, there's something for everyone.

And, of course, in the name of trick-or-*treat*, we saved the best for last: the wide array of desserts that change with the season's theme. For Halloween, we savored a vanilla cupcake with orange chocolate shavings, along with one of the restaurant's classics, Mississippi Mud Pie. My kids especially enjoyed the soft-serve ice cream.

CHARACTER CAULDRONS OF FUN

After grabbing a delicious first course, the real magic arrived: the characters. Unlike quick character meet-and-greets elsewhere in the park, here you get to have a leisurely encounter with Minnie, Mickey, Goofy, and Pluto, all decked out in their Halloween best. It was pure delight to see them take their time interacting with everyone, especially the kids.

Our hostess, Minnie, looked like a dazzling Halloween queen in a vibrant purple-and-orange dress with spiderweb accents. Her witchy ensemble included a matching hat and flowing spiderweb cape. Mickey, ever the charmer, sported a spider-themed outfit, too, with dapper spider button details and his own webbed cape. Pluto sported a glittery bat collar that wagged excitedly with every greeting. Goofy, never one to miss a party theme, rounded out the crew as a cowboy with a spooky twist: a spider belt buckle and creepy-crawlies nestled in his hat.

The best part? Each character made two visits throughout our meal. This was a huge perk for the kids, who were buzzing with excitement each time. It's a key advantage of character dining; the interactions are much more personal and relaxed than quick park encounters with long lines. This was especially valuable for us, as my oldest son was a bit hesitant to leave his seat during Mickey's first visit. But the magic of multiple visits worked its charm! By the time Mickey came around again, my son was all smiles and eager to interact, making it a truly memorable experience for him — and for us. 🐭

Tina's kids meet Mickey.

ON THIS DAY IN DISNEY HISTORY...

OCT. 2, 2009

Magic Kingdom guests who visited the park on Oct. 2, 2009, witnessed a special parade. Disney Parks and NASA came together to celebrate the homecoming of Buzz Lightyear, a 12-inch action figure who spent more than a year onboard the International Space Station. The ticker-tape parade down Main Street featured a marching band and astronauts Buzz Aldrin (Lightyear's namesake) and Mike Fincke. Fincke had accompanied Buzz Lightyear onboard the space station.

OCT. 2, 2011

While there are currently 13 official Disney Princesses, Disney welcomed Rapunzel as the 10th in a celebration at Kensington Palace in London on Oct. 2, 2011. The nine other Disney Princesses at the time — Ariel, Aurora, Belle, Cinderella, Jasmine, Mulan, Pocahontas, Snow White, and Tiana — joined Rapunzel for her procession.

OCT. 11, 2013

In 2013, The ExtraTERRORestrial Alien Encounter — considered by many to be the scariest Disney World attraction ever created — officially closed. This horrifying attraction, in which guests were strapped into seats as an alien creature prowled the laboratory, was ultimately replaced by the more family-friendly Stitch's Great Escape!

OCT. 27, 2007

In celebration of the 13th anniversary of Tower of Terror, Disney hosted the special Tower of Terror 13K and 6.5K races on Oct. 27, 2007. The event included a post-race party that went until 1 a.m., plus a special medal: a detailed replica of the Hollywood Tower Hotel

Check out the full history archives online.

PHOTO BY CLIFF WANG

The Headless Horseman, Milky Ways, and Magic

A Solo Trip to Mickey's Not-So-Scary Halloween Party

By Cathy Salustri

For many, this Halloweentime event means rare character meets, fireworks, and all the candy you can carry. But for me, it's about the Headless Horseman, quiet moments in a crowded park, and time to find hidden magic.

My passion for Halloween is a birthright. That's not hyperbole; I was born in Sleepy Hollow. Yes, it's a real village on the Hudson River, and it has a real bridge much like the one used in its namesake movies. That's because Washington Irving, who wrote the short story, lived in that Dutch-American community. He's also buried in the cemetery that factors prominently in the American version of the legend.

In case my surname doesn't give it away, I'm not Dutch, but until I was 4, we lived near Sleepy Hollow, in Ossining. Since leaving New York, I've revisited Sleepy Hollow only twice, but the legend of the Headless Horseman intrigues me: While different iterations of the story date to the Middle Ages and King Arthur, in the Sleepy Hollow telling, the Horseman's a German soldier who fought for the British in the Revolutionary War; during battle, a cannonball decapitated him. Every night, his headless ghost re-creates his final battle, with the Horseman returning to his grave each dawn.

My mom first told me of the legend before any live-action Sleepy Hollow films existed. She could tell me the story, I could read it myself, or I could watch *The Adventures of Ichabod and Mr. Toad*. I didn't need the Tim Burton version to make me fall in love with this beheaded incubus; I was besotted at an early age.

Most kids had Little Golden Books a la *Poky Little Puppy* or *The Monster at the End of This Book*, and in all fairness to my mom and dad, I had those, too, but my favorite children's story was the one that pretend-scared me about a wooden bridge, a pumpkin head, and a Headless Horseman. In retrospect, this explains quite a bit about me.

We're a family of December birthdays (dad, Dec. 7; mom, Dec. 9; and me, Dec. 14), so my parents knew December birthdays could get co-opted by Christmas. Maybe that's why, as far back as I remember, they paid special attention to pre-Christmas holidays. My parents made sure that, no matter how tight money was, I had a proper

The real Sleepy Hollow. **PHOTO BY CATHY SALUSTRI** | *PREVIOUS: Welcome to the party.* **PHOTO BY LAURIE SAPP**

Halloween costume: Raggedy Ann, a witch, Peter Pan, and a host of 1980s-style plastic masks, held in place with elastic that would no doubt break sometime during trick-or-treating (usually before you suffocated under the plastic). Christmas, Thanksgiving, and birthdays were consumed with large Italian family gatherings, but Halloween was always only the three of us.

So it's my parents on my mind as I wander through opening night of Mickey's Not-So-Scary Halloween Party. My husband opted to stay back at Disney's Port Orleans Resort - Riverside with our hellhounds, some quiet time, and a prime rib with his name on it at Boatwrights, but not me.

Nope, I'm here in Liberty Square, giddy as I wait for the Headless Horseman.

Lines for the Mickey pumpkin popcorn bucket are so long you'd think Disney had brought back the Figment bucket, the Minnie-as-Winnie Sanderson Sister sipper is more coveted than a Club 33 membership, and when the marshmallow foam machine temporarily goes down at Pinocchio Village Haus, I fear these gentle guests may riot. But I don't care about any of that: I want the Horseman.

For many Disney fans, the Headless Horseman ushers in the Halloween season.
PHOTO BY LAURIE SAPP

In addition to the Headless Horseman, the parade features a number of favorites, including Constance Hatchaway, Mickey, and Powerline Max. In between parades and stages shows, wander the park to load up on candy.
PHOTOS BY LAURIE SAPP

CHEERS!

Boo Raspberry Slushy

Story by Cathy Salustri
Photo by Laurie Sapp

A fter a not-as-long-as-you'd-expect wait on opening night of Mickey's Not-So-Scary Halloween Party, I watched doubtfully as the Cast Member handed me a purple-foam-topped blue drink: the Boo Raspberry Slushy, one of the party-exclusive beverages.

What purple foods grow in nature? I tried to think. *No way Disney put eggplant in this slushy.* I needn't have worried (although I am a huge fan of the nightshade); the floof of marshmallow foam tasted nothing like my eggplant parm. The drink, which, at first sight, made my brain shriek,

"SUGAR HIGH!" Haunted Mansion-style, actually fell lower on the "grab your Metformin" scale than expected. The marshmallow ghost looked and tasted suspiciously like the Peeps variety I use in my Peep-O-Ween cake every Halloween. It was arguably the sweetest part of the drink; I literally gave up the ghost after two bites. The indigo-colored, raspberry-flavored slush underneath the foamy aubergine mountain of mallow elicited memories of long summer days when friends and I would walk to the corner store and get a blue Slush Puppie in a waxed paper cup, circa 1983.

After a few slurps of foam — unless you bring your own smoothie straw, there's no way you're getting all that marshmallow through a traditional Disney one — I scooped most of it off and drank up the good stuff. It hit every bit as much at Pinocchio's Village Haus as it did right outside the Convenient store in Clearwater, Florida, on a hot August day.

Is a 30-second Headless Horseman ride through Liberty Square worth $150? For this woman, absolutely. Last year, I remember the Headless Horseman galloping past me; this year, he takes his time, and his measured not-quite-trot through Liberty Square feels delicious.

After the parade ends, I wander through the park, alone with my thoughts and a little down that for me, the best part has ended. Last year, I headed to the party weeks after my dad died unexpectedly. I wasn't in the right frame of mind to enjoy it.

This year, my mom's going through chemotherapy for breast cancer, and while her prognosis isn't terminal, she's not tolerating the chemo as well as her doctor had hoped. Mainly, she's not eating. Without a companion there to distract me from the voices in my head, my thoughts turn to her. For two weeks following each treatment, it would be easier to get a toddler to swallow brussels sprouts than to get my mom to eat enough calories. Seeing your mom sick is scary. Not the good pretend-scared of the menacing Headless Horseman, but the kind of scared a kid gets when they face a new, very real, fear.

"Come on, Mom, how often will a doctor tell you to eat whatever you want, as much as you want?" I'd begged her after the first round of chemo. Resultantly, she's developed a chemo-induced affinity for Milky Ways.

As I wander solo through Magic Kingdom, a light appears in the distance. Not a metaphorical one over my head, but a light-up

Cathy wanders the party in search of Milky Ways and the Headless Horseman. **PHOTO BY LAURIE SAPP**

inflatable that indicates a MNSSHP candy stop. *I'm going to get my mom all the candy,* I think to myself.

And I do. Forget Haunted Mansion or Big Thunder or meeting Jack and Sally: I'm now officially here to gather treats for my mom. Cast Members stand at the ready, scooping a sugar cornucopia of chocolate, gummy, and sour treats into my bag. That's the reason I find myself wandering through Mickey's PhilharMagic Concert, one of this year's candy stops. As I enter, a candy-laden Cast Member tells me I'll only see shorts tonight, not the regular attraction. No 3D glasses, no special effects, no snoozing Donald, just...

No way. It can't be.

During the party, you can catch classic cartoons instead of Mickey's PhilharMagic. **PHOTO BY CATHY SALUSTRI**

The Legend of Sleepy Hollow. The 1949 animated version, complete with narration from Bing Crosby, the groundbreaking multiplane animation, and all the mid-century magic of Walt Disney Studios. I stare at the screen, transfixed, and sit down in the dead center of the theater. I haven't seen this film in more than 40 years, and it's every bit as wonderful as it was the last time I watched it.

I'm sitting on my knees on the multi-colored carpeted floor in my aunt's den. My dad is still alive, my mom is healthy, and I have not a care in the world as I watch poor Ichabod muddle his way through colonial Sleepy Hollow. I can hear my mom and dad talking with the grown-ups in the other room, and yes, the Headless Horseman has some undertones of Chernabog, but 8-year-old me has nothing real to fear. Life is good. Being pretend-scared is kinda fun, actually.

The cartoon ends, the credits roll, and I'm back in the Concert Hall.

As *The Skeleton Dance,* Walt's first *Silly Symphony,* starts to play, I take my leave of the theater and look for the next candy station, my mood lighter and a twist of hope in my heart. Was it serendipity that brought me to the theater and back to the safe haven of my childhood, or coincidence? Was my dad trying to send me a message of love and hope from beyond the veil, or Walt Disney Imagineering trying to find a way to entertain tired partygoers in an air-conditioned theater?

I choose to chalk it up to magic. Whether it's Disney or Divine, though, I'll take it. 🐭

BOO TO YOU... AND YOU... AND YOU... (AND YOU GET THE IDEA — COME ALONG WITH US!)

MAIN STREET CONFECTIONERY

MARS
YELLOW
M&M'S Milk Chocolate

MARS
LIGHT BLUE
M&M'S MILK CHOCOLATE CANDIES

MARS
ELECTRIC GREEN
M&M'S MILK CHOCOLATE CANDIES

MARS
DARK GREEN
M&M'S MILK CHOCOLATE CANDIES

MARS
DARK PINK
M&M'S MILK CHOCOLATE CANDIES

MARS
GREEN
M&M'S MILK CHOCOLATE CANDIES

TOP 5
Candy Hauls Around Walt Disney World

BY TRISHA DAAB

You don't have to trick-or-treat at Walt Disney World to fill a pillowcase (or blue Disney Parks bag) with candy. Follow your nose to these five spots for a sweet candy haul.

M&M's, Disney Springs West Side

These thin-candy-shell nuggets of chocolatey goodness are classic. Print your face or Wu-Tang Clan name on it, or create a custom blend to match your DisneyBound for a unique sugar rush. Be a foolish mortal and mix teal peanut, purple and black milk, and green and white mint for a Haunted Mansion blend. Come here for the candy, but stay for the atmosphere and other goodies: The M&M's store has exclusive merchandise, a yellow M&M outside perfect for a selfie, and a rainbow wall of candy to marvel at.

Disney's Candy Cauldron, Disney Springs West Side

Disney Springs is also home to Disney's Candy Cauldron, with the standard sugar-rush-inducing bulk candy, packaged candy, lollipops, and the latest specialty apples, like the Halloween Poison Apple. In fact, a statue of The Queen, as the old peddler woman in *Snow White and the Seven Dwarfs*, will tempt you to *go on*, have a bite of a freshly made candy-coated apple. Not hungry? You can still drool and watch as the Cast Members create sugary concoctions in the show kitchen.

Zuri's Sweets Shop, Disney's Animal Kingdom

Across from the Kilimanjaro Safaris entrance is Zuri's Sweets Shop. Zuri's has all the usual sweet suspects: packaged candy, candy-coated popcorn, and the typical bakery case items. Specialty and seasonal treats also pop up here, including Halloween treats such as the Mickey pumpkin caramel apple. Since opening in 2015, Zuri's has offered different treats inspired by animals in the kingdom — giraffe and tiger iced cookies, zebra tail marshmallow pops, and the adorable monkey head caramel apple. The most recent too-cute-to-eat treat? The Hippo Wand — marshmallows dipped in cookie crumbs with a hippo face.

Main Street Confectionery, Magic Kingdom

Walt Disney World's original candy store has wafted sugary sweet smells down Main Street, U.S.A. since opening day. At the end of a long park day, wait out the mass exodus here. Bus lines are much better when munching on fresh cotton candy or fudge. The Confectionery has all the essentials: candy-coated treats, packaged candy, and candy popcorn, which you can customize at Kernel Kitchen. Many of Disney's flavored popcorns are created by Popcorn Junkie, a family-owned Orlando company. Walt Disney and the founder of Popcorn Junkie have more than a love of popcorn in common: They're both originally from Chicago!

Mitsukoshi Department Store, EPCOT

You don't need to board a plane for Japanese candy; follow your sweet tooth to the Mitsukoshi Department Store in EPCOT's Japan Pavilion. Chew gummies galore with muscat and peach flavors; tear into a bag of Japanese Pop Rocks; decide if Hello Kitty chocolate marshmallows are too cute to eat; or try one of the nearly 300 varieties of Kit Kats from Japan, such as chocolate orange and strawberry. Pocky is where it's at with fun flavors like banana, matcha, and coconut, or test your taste buds back home with Tamagogani — dried little crabs coated in starch, soy, mirin, and sugar.

The M&M wall at Main Street Confectionery. **PHOTO BY JUDD HELMS**

WORLD CELEBRATION

COMPLETING EPCOT'S TRANSFORMATION

BY STEPHANIE SHUSTER

Ll things must grow and evolve; no one was a firmer believer in that than Walt Disney himself. To wit, throughout the past five years, Walt Disney Imagineering has undertaken the massive challenge of updating a park whose essence is looking to the future, while respecting the past. The completion of EPCOT's World Celebration earlier this year marked the end of this (current) transformation.

"Walt's vision of EPCOT ... is an incredible vision, especially, I think, in this day and age, about community, about celebrating cultures and diversity, music, and art from around the world," said Bruce Vaughn, Chief Creative Officer, Walt Disney Imagineering, at the official opening ceremony for World Celebration. "And here, where we have restored the heart of EPCOT ... we have a new place where we can continue to do that in ways we haven't before."

Bruce Vaughn and Auli'i Cravalho deliver the opening remarks for the first reveal of a completed World Celebration. **PHOTO BY DANNY SHUSTER**

THE FUTURE (WORLD) IS IN THE PAST

When EPCOT opened, the park was divided into two halves: Future World focused on science and technology, and World Showcase served as a permanent World's Fair. Originally, the central area of Future World was a plaza stretching from Spaceship Earth toward World Showcase, flanked by the semicircular CommuniCore East and West buildings, and anchored by the Fountain of Nations in the middle. Through the years, these spaces were home to shopping, dining, character meet-and-greets, entertainment, and attractions — a truly multipurpose hub in the heart of the park.

According to Bruce, Imagineers have "restored the heart of EPCOT" with World Celebration. **PHOTO BY DANNY SHUSTER**

> ## "One of the big goals was giving park back to the park."

After five years of transformation, however, EPCOT has retired the name Future World and rebranded the front half of the park into three new neighborhoods, whose naming conventions match World Showcase: World Discovery to the east, World Nature to the west, and, in the center, World Celebration, which completed its transformation this spring. World Celebration has completely reimagined the center of EPCOT, and as Brianna Pfost, Creative Director, Walt Disney Imagineering, told us, "One of the big goals was giving park back to the park."

PREVIOUS: Welcome to World Celebration. | RIGHT: Look for intricate design details throughout this new space. **PHOTOS BY DANNY SHUSTER**

The newly opened CommuniCore Hall. **PHOTO BY DANNY SHUSTER**

Today, Dreamers Point anchors the new area, named for its Walt the Dreamer statue, which looks out over the area, across EPCOT, and to the future. If you stand by Walt and look toward World Showcase, to your left you'll see the new Connections Cafe and Eatery and the Creations Shop, connected by a breezeway, which also houses Club Cool, an enduring Future World staple. To your right stands CommuniCore Hall; its name an homage to the opening-day CommuniCore Pavilion, this building serves as a flexible space for EPCOT's events and festivals and houses the Mickey & Friends meet-and-greet. Head through CommuniCore Hall to a peaceful lawn area and new stage with a changing roster of entertainment (such as *¡Celebración Encanto!*, which debuted this summer). Last, turn your gaze to the center of the space to see the World Celebration Gardens.

The stage at CommuniCore Plaza will host various shows throughout the year, such as this Encanto-themed show that debuted with the opening of World Celebration. **PHOTO BY DANNY SHUSTER**

World Celebration is an area to slow down, relax, and connect with loved ones amid a busy park day. **PHOTO BY DANNY SHUSTER**

The gardens are divided into quadrants — each featuring different landscaping, seating, lighting, and design elements that give them distinct but united personalities. The northeast corner feels like an extension of Connections Cafe with patio lounge chairs; the southeast features meandering paths to explore; the southwest has abundant seating (including outlets and charging ports); and the northwest is a sculpture garden that hides some of the necessary tech for live shows and other entertainment in this new space.

FORM AND FUNCTION

Before Imagineers could transform this section of EPCOT into World Celebration, they first had to agree on what makes EPCOT, EPCOT. They considered patterns, shapes, and material design choices popular during EPCOT's early days, and then modernized these concepts to create a brighter, more open, and organic flow.

"We took off the heavy walls, we replaced [them] with glass, and we tried to make it transparent," Scott Mallwitz, Executive Creative Director, Walt Disney Imagineering, told *WDW Magazine* during an exploration of the gardens.

"Standing in Connections, you can see out into the gardens and into the spaces, and you do get that sense of transparency and diminishing of barriers that we wanted," Brianna added. "And then, when it becomes dark, you can stand right here in this area, and you can see all the way into that beautiful mural in Connections ... You don't feel the building anymore; you just feel a continued sense of environment."

EPCOT also has a beautiful symmetry that Imagineers preserved in the reimagining.

"If you start at the top of the Spaceship Earth panels, and you follow it, the center seam, all the way down to the center seam of the windows, to the center seam of the City of Progress and the bench to the center of the hardscape — follow that down to the center of the logo planter that lines up perfectly with the flag in America," Brianna explained. "Perfectly symmetrical."

But don't let the heavy hand of architectural design fool you: This space is lush and green thanks to more than 300 trees Imagineers planted.

"We added almost an acre of green space," Doug Tobin, Landscape Architect, Walt Disney Imagineering, told us. "If you remember what was here before, it was like a concrete jungle, right? So this is welcoming; this is an acre of usable green space."

According to Doug, each garden has its own personality — something his team prioritized when imagining the gardens in their design workshops. Brianna also told us the World Celebration Gardens will grow and change over time, transforming with each season and festival.

For many fans, a night at EPCOT isn't complete without a stroll over magical illuminated pavement, originally achieved with fiber optics embedded in the concrete of Future World. Imagineers wanted to retain that sense of wonder but used LEDs to create a starfield at Walt the Dreamer and to illuminate the EPCOT logo in the center of the gardens. It has all the same programming functionality as the Beacons of Magic installation on Spaceship Earth so it can glow with the show or be customized for private events.

"Nothing here doesn't have a purpose," Scott said of World Celebration. "It all is purposefully and mindfully created so that we can support what's going on."

The new area preserves EPCOT's symmetry. **PHOTO BY LAURIE SAPP**

Watch the space transform at night.
PHOTO BY DANNY SHUSTER

And stick around for a unique view of the fireworks. **PHOTO BY LAURIE SAPP**

The nighttime lighting transforms the area.
PHOTO BY CLIFF WANG

Like anywhere else at Walt Disney World, there's every bit as much magic looking down as there is looking up. **PHOTO BY LAURIE SAPP**

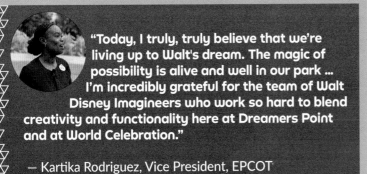

"Today, I truly, truly believe that we're living up to Walt's dream. The magic of possibility is alive and well in our park ... I'm incredibly grateful for the team of Walt Disney Imagineers who work so hard to blend creativity and functionality here at Dreamers Point and at World Celebration."

— Kartika Rodriguez, Vice President, EPCOT

FROM NOSTALGIA TO WHAT'S NEXT

For Imagineers, Walt was always the center of the story of World Celebration.

"It's important to put Walt here and think about ... what he brought to Central Florida," said Scott at the unveiling of the Walt the Dreamer statue on Walt's birthday in 2023.

Imagineers researched every detail of this revitalized area. In wandering the gardens, Scott encouraged guests to look down: "You're going to see many details that are driven up from some of those early planning documents, some of the early architecture of our original pavilions, the materiality, the pattern, the color of the shape. We're going to continue to celebrate those things. And it's all intrinsically EPCOT. You are in no other place but in the heart of EPCOT."

Imagineers also carefully considered Walt's pose where he sits at Dreamers Point: "We knew from the onset that we wanted to place [Walt] in a point in time, very close to when the Florida film was announced, very close to that Sunday night broadcast," Scott told us. "And so we began to mine out all the imagery, all the photography, story sessions, public relations things, trips with Lillian — just everything we can to create a big board and say, 'OK, this is what he looked like. This is the suit he had, the kind of shoes he wore ... this is how he *felt*."

Imagineers always knew Walt would be central to World Celebration. **PHOTO BY JUDD HELMS**

THE TOMORROW TOWER SUITE
EPCOT may already have The Seas Pavilion, but the park's aesthetic will hit the high seas later this year. The *Disney Treasure* sets sail in December, and it features a futuristic funnel suite that captures many of the same design choices as EPCOT's makeover. The two-story Concierge Suite is a one-of-a-kind, luxury space that can sleep up to eight.

CONCEPT ART ©DISNEY

Imagineers designed the statue to show Walt "optimistic" and "accessible," so guests can "share that moment with him" when they visit the area. **PHOTO BY LAURIE SAPP**

Sit for a bit to enjoy the new architectural details, fragrant flowers, and evocative soundtrack. **PHOTO BY JUDD HELMS**

For Scott and the Imagineers, the statue needed to set the tone for World Celebration and the entire park.

"We want him to be optimistic, and we want him to be accessible," explained Scott, so Imagineers positioned him "slightly leaning forward, with a little bit of a smile on his face, just appreciating the day... and the fact that you can share that moment with him was a key driver to this position."

The final sprinkle of pixie dust on this new area? A soundtrack to rival the iconic original background music of Future World. The new loop features orchestrations of the EPCOT theme composed by Pinar Toprak (*Captain Marvel*), who also contributed to the score for *Luminous*. It's melodic, evocative, peaceful, and inspiring all at once.

In reflecting on the ultimate purpose of World Celebration, Scott said, "The memories that you share for decades after are the moments in between the attractions," not simply the attractions

themselves. The laughs you have and the discoveries you make as you wander paths or sit and relax with friends and family.

Thus, World Celebration is a "space for people to invent their own connection ... That's what this is about."

LET'S WALK THROUGH THIS
WHOLE NEW WORLD.

Biergarten Restaurant

Where Every Day is Oktoberfest

By Timothy Moore

Biergarten offers an authentic German experience with delicious food, live music, and immersive theming.

The first Oktoberfest included a horse race and a royal wedding — but no beer tents. Since that inaugural celebration in 1810, the party's gotten decidedly more beer-focused, with millions of locals and tourists flooding the streets of Munich each fall to don their lederhosen and raise a stein to good health and good fortune.

Last month, I had the opportunity to experience a true Oktoberfest in Munich for the first time, but I already felt like a pro. After all, I'd had good practice at EPCOT's Biergarten Restaurant, where they celebrate Oktoberfest every day, no matter the season.

AN AUTHENTIC BAVARIAN VILLAGE

The Germany Pavilion offers an array of enticing entertainment. Wander into Karamell-Küche for some of the best sweets on Disney Property, shop for Christmas ornaments year-round at Die Weihnachts Ecke, and grab a grapefruit hefeweizen to take with you on your stroll into Italy (but don't forget to stop and watch the trains!). If you're in a hurry, you might miss this pavilion's hidden gem, set farther back: Biergarten Restaurant, a Table-Service all-you-can-eat buffet, where Advance Dining Reservations are highly recommended.

ABOVE, LEFT, & BELOW: A polka band performs sets throughout your meal. **PHOTOS BY ABBY RICHARDSON** | *BOTTOM LEFT: The exterior of the restaurant.* **PHOTO BY CLIFF WANG** | *NEXT PAGE: Soak up the atmosphere of a nighttime Oktoberfest celebration.* **PHOTOS BY ABBY RICHARDSON**

As soon as you set foot inside Biergarten from the Germany Pavilion, the wafting scent of sauerkraut transports you to another place. Look around and you'll notice that, though you're inside, Disney's designed the restaurant to feel like an outdoor, twilit biergarten. Your table, reflecting the kinds of communal tables you'd find in a true German biergarten, is set in an open-air platz, surrounded by multi-story Bavarian building facades that are quite true to a real German city center.

"If you visit Bavarian towns — for example, Bamberg or Rothenburg ob der Tauber — you'll find similar buildings in the densely built medieval city centers," René Zieprich, a German architect living in Leipzig, told me. "Two- or three-story houses with shops and stores on the first floor are common. You'll see ornate timber-framed facades and gabled roofs with a projecting hoist. Disney's version is simply more theatrical and romanticized."

> **"As soon as you set foot inside Biergarten from the Germany Pavilion, the wafting scent of sauerkraut transports you to another place."**

All around the restaurant are subtle signs that you're outside in a Bavarian village during Oktoberfest. An orange-leafed tree beside an operating watermill signals the autumn season, and the restaurant is lit by lampposts (and the full moon hanging in the night sky). The floor is made of outdoor patio tiles, and wrought-iron railings separate the various levels of the restaurant. According to René, Imagineers have done a tremendous job at creating a true biergarten atmosphere inside the restaurant.

The tables at EPCOT's Biergarten form a tiered half-circle surrounding the central stage, where a polka band plays 25-minute sets throughout the night. During my meal, I saw a couple of sets, which included music from the alpenhorn (picture those long horns from the Ricola commercials) and several other brass and woodwind instruments. The band also played an accordion, guitar, and cowbells — and got plenty of guests on their feet dancing in front of the stage.

IT'S JÄGER TIME

The largest beer at Walt Disney World might just be at Biergarten. Here, you can order German beers by the half liter *or*, if you're adventurous, by the liter. And when in Bavaria, do as the Bavarians do, right?

I kicked off my meal with a full liter of the Warsteiner Dunkel, a dark pilsner with rich chocolate aromas and a deep, caramel taste. At a real Oktoberfest, people drink these all day, but here in EPCOT, one is more than enough, especially if you've had your fair share of drinks elsewhere around World Showcase throughout the day.

But something else on the menu caught my eye and took me back to my own family in Ohio. Our family has German roots, and it's been a long tradition at gatherings — Christmases, birthdays, graduation parties, or out-of-town relatives visiting — to share a round of Jägermeister.

Throughout each gathering, a thirsty family member might catch the eyes of a few others who aren't driving home at the end of the day and whisper, "Jäger time?" Anyone interested in another chilled shot of the black licorice liqueur will wander into the kitchen, where Grandpa stands ready to pour.

Remembering my grandfather and grandmother in Ohio — two of the world's biggest Disney fans who spent the last five decades making Walt Disney World their second home — I couldn't resist ordering a shot of Jäger and toasting my grandparents, the oompah music playing in the background as I celebrated my family's time-honored tradition.

A shot of Jägermeister takes Tim back to family gatherings, but he also ordered a pint of beer because, well, when in Germany... **PHOTOS BY ABBY RICHARDSON**

"The largest beer at Walt Disney World might just be at Biergarten."

A GERMAN FEAST

As much as I loved my liter of Dunkel and the nostalgic Jäger, I was here for the food. And what a spread Biergarten offers. You'll need several trips to the buffet to sample everything, and there's not a bad item on offer.

The pretzels are pillow-soft and great for dipping in the cheese and beer soup, a standout from the buffet, of which you'll likely want multiple bowls. The soup is creamy and hot, and the bacon makes it extra savory. Another German staple is potato salad; at Biergarten, the potato skin stays on, and the cold temperature is a nice contrast to the steaming soup.

But potato salad is only one way Biergarten prepares the potatoes. I was quite fond of the roasted potatoes, which were salty and fluffy (and another great option for dipping in the soup). Meat lovers will not go hungry here; Biergarten offers multiple preparations of sausage, all savory and well-cooked — and perfectly paired with the sweet sauerkraut. Because it's a buffet, you can get adventurous here with little consequence; I tried the liverwurst and, to my surprise, I quite enjoyed it. The pork roast was also tender and flavorful, but the pork schnitzel was a little tough and dry for my tastes. It could've just been a bad batch (or that it had been sitting out too long).

It's not all meat and potatoes, though. You'll get a balanced meal at Biergarten with German green beans (fresh and salty, with a hearty helping of garlic), bean salad, and a crisp and refreshing traditional salad, available with a mustard dressing. And don't miss the mac and cheese — it's crispy and crunchy on the outside, but holds pockets of savory, cheesy goodness on the inside.

The best part of a buffet, German or otherwise, is access to as many desserts as you'd like. I started with a German staple: the Black Forest cake. This delectable dessert was topped with sour cherries and chocolate shavings; you only need a few bites of this moist cake, which pairs well with an after-dinner coffee. I also sampled the blueberry crumble — tart, sweet, and fresh — and a gooey brownie with a pretzel on top.

AN AUTHENTIC BAVARIAN EXPERIENCE

EPCOT's Biergarten is one of the most immersive dining experiences I've had at Walt Disney World. From the faux architecture to the live music to the delicious food and drink that took me back to my German roots, Biergarten offers an authentic Bavarian experience in the heart of World Showcase.

EPCOT may seem like an odd place for a sit-down meal, given its near-constant festivals with food booths wherever you look, but if you have the time and like German food and good music, I recommend adding a meal here to your itinerary. Dunk your pretzel in the soup, clap your hands in time with the music, and raise your glass with a loud "Cheers!"

Or, as they say in Germany: *Prost!*

The buffet allows you to sample a wide range of German staples, including the popular cheese and beer soup and desserts such as Black Forest cake. **PHOTOS BY ABBY RICHARDSON**

OOMPAH! LET'S GET OUR POLKA ON.

Willkommen to EPCOT
Oktoberfest at the Germany Pavilion

BY MATTHEW KRUL

Celebrating the classic image of a German township, the Germany Pavilion at EPCOT pays homage to German culture, architecture, and cuisine. Drawing inspiration from German landmarks established between the 13th and 17th centuries, Imagineers worked to re-create an authentic Bavarian atmosphere, particularly in the Biergarten Restaurant, where guests can celebrate Oktoberfest all year long.

AN AUTHENTIC GERMAN PLATZ

With each World Showcase pavilion, Imagineers re-created instantly recognizable world landmarks and distinctive architecture so that guests could easily identify each country. Employing this design philosophy required careful research, as

Imagineers looked for unique and well-defined visual cues to mark individual national styles.

For the Germany Pavilion, Imagineers turned to a traditional German platz (plaza), similar to an American town square. Each element of the pavilion is inspired by a real German location. For example, the castle walls at the back of the plaza are inspired by Eltz Castle near Koblenz and Stahleck Fortress near Bacharach. Nearby, the Biergarten Restaurant entrance is inspired by a similar restaurant in Rothenburg ob der Tauber. Imagineers took additional inspiration from Freiburg, Rothenburg, and Römerburg Platz in Frankfurt to create the smaller facades.

ABOVE: The pavilion is a re-creation of a traditional German platz.
NEXT PAGE: A statue of St. George slaying a dragon from atop his steed. **PHOTOS BY CLIFF WANG**

These three statues are dedicated to Philip I, Charles V, and Ferdinand I, modeled after the original statues in Freiburg. **PHOTOS BY JUDD HELMS**

FINISHING TOUCHES

Beyond the building architecture, design pieces enhance the historic feel of the pavilion. For instance, the second-floor balcony of Gild Hall at the front of the pavilion features three statues dedicated to Philip I, Charles V, and Ferdinand I. These figures are modeled after those found at the Kaufhaus in Freiburg and represent the original Hapsburg emperors, a European family who ruled Austria-Hungary from 1273 to 1918 (missing is Maximilian I, who was removed from the pavilion to fit the size of the EPCOT location).

Meanwhile, the center of the courtyard features a statue of St. George, the patron saint of soldiers, slaying a dragon. While many German villages feature a similar statue, thought to be a symbol of protection, this particular statue is modeled after the one found in Rothenburg. According to German legend, St. George killed a dragon to save the king's daughter, and the folklore continues at EPCOT.

Another finishing touch at the pavilion is one that cannot be seen. The music playing in the background at the Germany Pavilion draws on traditional music from the region, including such iconic tunes as "Chromatic Polka" (Louis Köhler), "Minuet in G Major" (Christian Petzold), "Cradle Song" (Johannes Brahms), and a traditional Laendler Waltz.

AN OKTOBERFEST BIERGARTEN

Oktoberfest is one of the longest-running celebrations enjoyed in Germany today, a tradition that continues at the pavilion's only Table-Service restaurant. Unlike the exterior facades of the Germany Pavilion, the interior Biergarten space got a theatrical treatment, creating a twilight ambience that feels like something out of a Disney fairy tale.

Biergarten combines several cultural elements of Oktoberfest, including costumes, food, beverages, and music. While enjoying bratwurst, pork schnitzel, Bavarian cheesecake, and a wide

LOCATION:
Inside the Karamell-Küche store at the Germany Pavilion in EPCOT

DIFFICULTY:

Photos by Marisa Alvarado

range of drink options, a live polka band performs a 25-minute variety show that features traditional Oktoberfest music. From brass instruments to accordions and hand bells to alpenhorns, the show includes an assortment of instruments from the region. When it comes to the musical selections, no Oktoberfest would be complete without the classic song, "Ein Prosit der Gemütlichkeit," so sing along if you know the words.

CELEBRATING GERMAN CULTURE

As with all World Showcase pavilions, Disney strives to give guests a taste of the traditional customs, history, and cuisine of each pavilion's host country. Since opening day, the Germany Pavilion has done so with few changes. Whether grabbing a pretzel and a beer, savoring caramel popcorn, shopping for cuckoo clocks, or exploring the pavilion's miniature railroad set, you're bound to enjoy a German adventure at EPCOT.

A PUMPKIN PICK-ME-UP

From hippos to guinea pigs, tigers to rhinos, lemurs to hoofstock, the animals at Disney's Animal Kingdom rely on constant enrichment opportunities to keep them sharp and engaged. While the animal keepers have lots of tricks up their sleeves to challenge and entertain the species they care for, pumpkins are one of the most popular forms of enrichment each October.

"We love to provide pumpkins for our animals during the fall," said Angela Miller, Behavior Husbandry Zoological Manger, The Walt Disney Company, in a video for Disney Parks. "That gives our animals the opportunity to have a novel experience with them … Keepers really enjoy being able to carve them in unique ways."

So why is enrichment important, and why pumpkins?

"We use enrichment to actually give animals lots of different choices in their environment," Angela explained. "Some of the behaviors that we might anticipate seeing with animals could be foraging, so some animals will actually eat the pumpkins. Some animals are going to interact with them by shredding them. We want to make sure our animals have an opportunity to showcase their natural behaviors."

PHOTOS BY ANDY JERZEWSKI

MEET THE
MALAYAN FLYING FOX
WALT DISNEY WORLD'S RESIDENT BATS

BY TIMOTHY MOORE

The room was dark and still, filled with only the labored snores of our 220-pound Great Dane, Clyde, strategically snuggled in the dead center of the bed. But then — a pitter patter. No, a flutter. A flap maybe? Whatever it was, Clyde heard it, and, 220 pounds of pure strength or not, he was the first to bury himself deeper beneath the sheets and whimper.

"We have a bat in the house," Trent said, rolling out of bed and army-crawling to the wall, where he flipped on the light.

"We don't have a bat," I muttered through a yawn, rolling over to cuddle Clyde. "How would it get in?"

I have this thing, you see, where I'm always right — even when I'm not. But Trent was quick to tell me he left the attic window open by mistake, and whether I wanted to rub the sleep from my eyes and see it, a bat was currently dangling from our curtains and plotting its next move. Though I was terrified (and cowering under a blanket shroud), I sprang into action, helping Trent open one of our bedroom windows and determining how best to catch and release the bat. But as we tried to lead it to the open window, another bat

inadvertently swooshed in, circling our room chaotically like an alien swirling saucer.

It was a late night, but we eventually freed our home of both uninvited guests (and closed the attic window). As exhausting and frightening as it was to chase bats with a clear glass cup and strip of cardboard while avoiding their raining poos, I realized that night how fascinating these tiny, flying mammals were — and it started an animal passion I never expected.

Now, on every trip to Walt Disney World, no matter how brief my stay and how packed my itinerary, I make a point of visiting the Malayan flying foxes, the world's largest bat species, along the Maharajah Jungle Trek.

GOING TO BAT FOR BATS

Bats get a bad rep. Film, literature, and television paint them as blood-sucking menaces (who might turn us into vampires), and their close-quarters living does make it easy for them to spread diseases among their cauldrons — and then to humans. They're also nocturnal, which is inherently creepy; they sometimes emit an admittedly horrifyingly shrill screech; and, when magnified by the drinking glass you've

trapped them under to get them out of your bedroom, their fangs look deadlier than a tiger's.

But these creepy critters are also remarkably fascinating and important; many are pollinators and seed distributors. They're the only mammals to evolve powered flight, and they're the second-most diverse mammal species in the world (one in every five mammal species is a bat, and they live on every continent except Antarctica). Perhaps most intriguing is their echolocation, which allows them to pinpoint the precise location of an insect in the night sky and gobble it up, all without seeing it.

That last bit — echolocation — is a hallmark of most bat species, but not all of them. The bats at Walt Disney World, for example, don't use echolocation. Instead, their eyesight and sense of smell have developed enough that they can hunt prey using these more traditional senses — so much for "blind as a bat." In the wild, the Malayan flying foxes live in colonies of more than 250,000. If you brave the bat room along Maharajah Jungle Trek (Disney lets you bypass this room if you can't stomach the sight), you won't see a colony quite so large; this exhibit has 11 bats living together.

The flying foxes (don't let the name fool you; they're bats) enjoy a plethora of tree branches to roost from, caves for privacy and daytime naps, and a smorgasbord of fruit for snacking. Each day, these bats eat half their body weight in fruits and veggies, including bananas, pineapples, papayas, cucumbers, and carrots.

Malayan flying foxes are much larger than the typical bat. Some stand at more than a foot tall, and they can have a wingspan of more than 6 feet.

"Malayan flying foxes in southeast Asia help transport tree seeds that can reforest areas," says Dr. Mark Penning, Vice President of Animals, Science and Environment for Disney Parks, "and they are one of the few seed dispersers large enough to carry the seeds of many giant fruits in the area. They also consume insects, which help control disease."

Not ready to see the live bats at Animal Kingdom? Wet your toes with some faux bats dangling in the caverns of Big Thunder Mountain Railroad's first lift hill or on the moving platform as you board your Doom Buggy on Haunted Mansion.

Signage around the bat exhibit in Animal Kingdom suggests that some bats can eat up to 600 insects, including mosquitoes and other undesirable bugs, in an hour.

The International Union for Conservation of Nature lists large flying foxes as endangered; their main threat is habitat loss. The Disney Conservation Fund (DCF) continues to provide grants to protect animals and their habitats across the globe, including bats. A few years back, for instance, DCF awarded a grant to Bat

Conservation International (BCI) to slow and ultimately reverse the population decline of the Mexican long-nosed bat. DCF has also supported BCI in protecting golden-capped fruit bats in the Philippines and surveying the only known Fiji free-tailed bat maternity roost.

Beyond donating to the Disney Conservation Fund or to organizations like BCI directly, there are other ways people like you and I — people who care for these mammals, though we (and our giant dogs) may panic when they flap through our bedroom in the middle of the night — can protect bats. For instance, we can turn off unnecessary outdoor lights, as light pollution can disturb their nightly hunts. We can also leave dead and dying trees undisturbed if they're not causing an issue; these serve as ideal roosting spots for bats. We should avoid using pesticides in our yards; we may not like those bugs around our home, but hungry bats sure do (one bat can eat up to 3,000 bugs in a night). And if you have a green thumb, start a garden to attract pollinators that bats feed on (bonus — you'll promote healthy bee populations, too!).

A NEW APPRECIATION

Since that first encounter with bats in our home, Trent's and my appreciation for the mammal has only grown. The exhibit at Animal Kingdom is always inspiring, but our love for this creature became even more amplified following an amazing experience at Carlsbad Cavern National Park. Among a crowded amphitheater of respectfully silent hikers, we witnessed a voluminous vortex of thousands of bats blast out of the cave mouth and climb into the purpling sky in a swirl. Though I have no photographs to look back on (photos and video weren't allowed), it's one of the most crystal-clear travel memories I have: a tornado of hungry, flapping mammals ascending into the sky.

These creatures may give us the heebie-jeebies, but they're so spectacularly weird and beneficial to our world that you can't help but admire them. I've grown quite fond of these little guys, no longer panicking when I hear the flap of their wings or see them swooping toward their prey outside — though I still think we'll keep our attic window closed from now on. 🐭

MORE CREEPY CRITTERS

Though you can skip the bat room along Maharajah Jungle Trek, you'll still have to travel beneath giant bat kites dangling in the hallway. These are large — and might be more frightening than the actual bats in the exhibit.

I highly recommend peeking inside, and not only for the bats. Also on display are the tree monitor and the prehensile tailed skink, an adorable lizard that lives in the trees of Australian rainforests. Also in this room is one of the Wilderness Explorers checkpoints.

PREVIOUS: A bat hangs at Walt Disney World. LEFT: The floor as you enter and exit your Doom Buggy. **PHOTOS BY JUDD HELMS** | *TOP RIGHT: A bat kite near the exhibit. ABOVE: Bats hanging in their enclosure.* **PHOTOS BY CLIFF WANG** | *BELOW: A sign points the way to Maharajah Jungle Trek.* **PHOTO BY DANNY SHUSTER**

A tarantula at Conservation Station.

Discovering New Magic

MEET THE SPIDERS AND SCORPIONS OF ANIMAL KINGDOM

Story by Johnaé De Felicis | Photos by Cliff Wang

On a recent trip to Disney's Animal Kingdom, I untangled a common misconception about some invertebrates (like certain spider species) that slightly eased my fears of them. These eight-legged creatures don't simply exist to freak us out. Though creepy, spiders, such as crab spiders and jumping spiders, benefit our food supply.

Spiders receive partial credit for securing a healthy ecosystem by playing the role of pollinator, as they indirectly transfer pollen between plants while lurking for food. It's sort of a big deal, since we wouldn't have three-fourths of our plants or 35% of our crops without the planet's pollinators doing their jobs. That's right: We humans would be in a pinch if pollinators didn't exist.

In our plant food supply — where weeds and ruthless pests can destroy our crops — pollinators do us a huge favor by devouring crop-destroying insects. Spiders, it turns out, have a special place in this world after all.

I stood in amazement (and slight fear) while touring the Conservation Station at Animal Kingdom, hearing these and other scorpion and spider tidbits from Cast Members stationed near an invertebrates exhibit.

The web of truth doesn't stop spinning there, folks. Spiders and scorpions have their fair share of unique quirks, and the Conservation Station sheds light on what's often buried underneath the surface about these feared arachnids.

IN SEARCH OF ARACHNIDS

Near Kilimanjaro Safaris in Harambe, Africa, you'll find a well-covered train station where you can board the Wildlife Express Train. This train takes you to the Conservation Station — home to some of the park's invertebrates.

On the seven-minute train ride, you'll journey past the park's animal housing and veterinary areas. The train then drops you off at Rafiki's Planet Watch, and you'll take a short stroll through a scenic Habitat Habit! trail (with Rafiki leading the way) before arriving at the Conservation Station.

I enjoyed weaving my way through that peaceful pathway to our destination. The shady plants surrounding the path were a pleasant shield from the heat. It added a relaxing touch to the start of this creepy-crawly adventure.

Upon reaching the Conservation Station, I saw a petting zoo, a drawing class, and a couple of other animal exhibits that included a veterinary treatment room, as well as amphibian and reptile exhibits. But I was here for spiders and scorpions.

I set my arachnophobia aside to learn all that I could about these interesting invertebrates, starting with the spiders.

EIGHT-LEGGED CREEPY-CRAWLIES

Did you know southern house spiders (*Kukulcania hibernalis*) produce white webbing due to a silk-producing organ under their spinnerets (called the cribellium) and a special set of hairs on their feet (called calamistrum)? Or that the Cameroon red baboon spider (*Hysterocrates gigas*) has a knack for creating burrows? Neither did I, until I received a mini-science lesson from a slideshow about these spiders near the exhibit. I also learned that spiders don't have ears; they detect sound by feeling vibrations with the hairs on their legs.

Spiders either reside on high-rise webs or are "bottom dwellers" who mostly stay on the ground. But here at the Animal Kingdom exhibit, they also live behind glass windows — a reassuring note for those of us with arachnophobia.

A Cast Member also told me spiders don't keep their same exoskeleton forever; they molt, meaning they routinely shed that outer layer throughout their lifetime. And how they molt is especially intriguing. They do it by flipping over and lying on their backs, pushing off the exoskeleton with their legs. Talk about freaky!

And spiders can also shed their fangs, the Cast Member told me. Disney keeps some of the molts on display at the exhibit, giving passersby a frightening glimpse of a molt's actual appearance.

To support their molting process, Disney keeps a humidifier in the room. Apparently, a successful molting process requires a humid environment.

"When they're getting ready to molt, they need to have enough moisture on their body to be able to pull off their whole exoskeleton," the Cast Member explained.

STINGERS IN THE SPOTLIGHT
I also sharpened my knowledge about scorpions at the invertebrates exhibit. For instance, I learned desert hair scorpions (*Hadrurus arizonensis*) are North America's largest scorpion species. And I'm not exaggerating, either. These stingers can grow up to 14 centimeters (or approximately 5.5 inches). They were one of few scorpion species on display at the Conservation Station, along with the emperor scorpion (*Pandinus imperator*), which is also on the larger end.

What I learned about scorpions on this trip made me even more terrified of them, like how their venom can severely damage one's neurologic, cardiac, and respiratory systems. But fortunately, there's only a small chance that a scorpion's sting can kill; only 0.27% of their stings lead to death. I also learned that scientists experiment with their venom in hopes of finding new disease cures and treatments.

Oh, and one more thing: Scorpions are viviparous — so they don't lay eggs. Instead, they give birth to live young. One thing's for sure: These little critters are full of surprises!

ENTANGLED IN OUR ECOSYSTEM
Invertebrates: We can't live without them. They may terrify some of us (this writer included!), but they're a necessary part of society. Fortunately, the Disney Conservation Fund is focused on protecting these invertebrates, leading a collective community effort to preserve this special population by providing them with a comfortable habitat that supports their strengths. 🐭

See the spiders' molts on display.

You can also learn about scorpions here.

 RAFIKI'S PLANET WATCH HONORS ALL CREATURES, NO MATTER HOW MANY LEGS THEY HAVE

A charcuterie board at Maria & Enzo's often includes products from Orlando-area farms. **PHOTO BY PATINA RESTAURANT GROUP**

A Taste of Florida, A Taste of Italy

Eating Local at Maria & Enzo's

By Timothy Moore

Simply because you've left MCO and shuttled to Walt Disney World doesn't mean you're done with airports. One of the best meals on property awaits at Maria & Enzo's Ristorante at Disney Springs, a Sicilian restaurant set in a reclaimed airline terminal from the 1930s and helmed by Executive Chef Ben Dodaro.

Chef Ben emphasizes the importance of making true Sicilian (and, more broadly, Italian) cuisine, with flavors that might challenge visitors' perceptions of Italian food, especially if they've grown up eating Americanized versions of Italian classics. And in crafting a menu of authentic Sicilian dishes, Ben also strives to bring as much fresh Florida produce to the table as he can.

"If I can get something that I know is fresh and organic — and support a local farmer — I'll for sure do that," Chef Ben tells *WDW Magazine*.

A SICILIAN MENU WITH FLORIDA FLAVORS

The menu at Maria & Enzo's offers something for everyone. Chef Ben says the ravioli, spaghetti and meatballs, and chicken parmesan are among the most popular dishes — and great if you want the Italian standards you know. But the menu is also packed with his take on classic Sicilian dishes.

"Sicilian is a lot more tomato sauce; a lot more spice; a lot more citrus," Ben explains. "It's what you would find growing in that region. My family's from Calabria, so I love spicy pork and sausages, and I always try to incorporate that into the menu."

And the tomato sauce? It might not be what you expect.

"Everybody's used to a ton of garlic," Chef Ben says. "They often feel like tomato sauce should have a lot of herbs, onion powder, garlic powder. Our marinara sauce is very simple and more true to Sicilian tradition. It's olive oil, garlic, onions, really nice tomatoes — we use the San Marzano — and salt."

Chef Ben says that fresh ingredients are key to the success of not only this sauce, but all the dishes on the menu. Like other restaurants on property, Maria & Enzo's sometimes works with larger, commercial suppliers as needed. But whenever Ben can incorporate produce from local farmers, he will.

"We buy from Sugar Top Farms, which is a local farm," he says. The yields from Sugar Top Farms, 38 miles from Disney Springs in Clermont, will vary with the season. When we spoke in the winter, Chef Ben was getting a lot of tomatoes, arugula, microgreens, baby carrots, and broccolini. Now that it's fall, Ben will incorporate more autumnal vegetables from Sugar Top Farms and other nearby farmers into his menu. For instance, one of his favorite dishes is the Torchio Alle Verdure, a vegetable pasta that changes throughout the year, depending on what's being harvested.

"It's all seasonal vegetables," he says. "In the fall, we do mushrooms, roasted Brussels sprouts, sun-dried tomatoes, basil, and cipollini onion. We've even done roasted cauliflower and butternut squash for autumn."

This dish, and how it changes with the harvests, is only the tip of the iceberg. When farmers come in with something new or in season, it allows Chef Ben to create on the fly, or try unique substitutions in any of his long-standing menu items.

"We especially become more adventurous with some of the specials we run," Chef Ben says. "And that's all thanks to the fresh produce the local farmers bring in."

SWEET AS HONEY

Chef Ben relies on more than Orlando-grown fruits and vegetables to bring his menu to life. One of his more intriguing partners is Petal Honey Co., an Orlando-area, family-owned business that specializes in raw, unfiltered, single-source-origin honey, produced by bees on Florida farms, all sold in reusable glass containers.

"If I can get something that I know is fresh and organic — and support a local farmer — I'll for sure do that."

ABOVE: Visit Maria & Enzo's throughout the year to see how some dishes, such as Torchio Alle Verdure, change along with the seasons' fresh vegetables. LEFT: Chef Ben Dodaro. **PHOTOS BY PATINA RESTAURANT GROUP**

"If we bottle the honey as single origin from one farm, then we allow the honey to be nuanced by the season ... And I believe that's the healthiest honey you can get."

ABOVE & PREVIOUS: Petal Honey is a family-owned operation that produces raw, unfiltered, single-source-origin honey — which you can often find on the menu at Maria & Enzo's. **PETAL HONEY PHOTOS COURTESY OF POOLBOY STUDIO**

Drew Miller, the founder and operator of Petal Honey, dropped in to Maria & Enzo's one day and struck up a conversation with Chef Ben about the bees his family keeps and the honey they produce. At the time, Drew's family was already providing honey for another Disney Springs restaurant, Polite Pig, and he was looking to expand.

"We hit it off right away," Chef Ben says of Drew, a hard-working family man with a long beard and passion for natural beekeeping. "The honey's great, and the flavor changes seasonally. When Drew told me it was single-origin honey, I said, 'Wow, you have one bee making all this honey?' It was a stupid joke, but he appreciated it. I guess he likes dad jokes, too, and I knew right then he'd be a good match for the restaurant."

Although honey isn't common in Italian cuisine, Chef Ben says it's the perfect accompaniment for the Salumi e Formaggi, a charcuterie board of meats and cheeses. Chef Ben also created a specialty sweet-and-spicy pizza for Pizza Ponte last year during Disney Springs' Flavors of Florida, and Drew's honey was the star player.

The honey was a great addition to the sweet-and-spicy pizza. **PHOTO BY PATINA RESTAURANT GROUP**

"We did kind of a sweet-and-savory play, with spicy Calabrian salami and the sweet honey, plus tomato, pecorino cheese, and fresh basil," Chef Ben explains.

Ben continues to look for unique ways to incorporate honey into the menu. As it stands, the restaurant goes through two 60-pound buckets a month.

You can still find Petal's delicious honey at Polite Pig as well, and you can also get a taste at EPCOT. Space 220 serves a moist honey cake called The Astra, with honey sourced from Petal's Orlando bees. Beyond Disney, you'll find Petal Honey at several Orlando restaurants and retailers (you can also order jars of the honey or adopt a hive online, directly on Petal's website).

Get This Honey →

The Central Florida climate allows Petal to chase several different nectar flows each year. That means Drew and his family move their bees around to various farms as the seasons change: orange blossoms in the winter, then spring wildflower and palmetto in the spring and early summer, and a late-season wildflower through September. That late-season wildflower yields the honey you'll find at Maria & Enzo's, Polite Pig, and Space 220 this fall and into the winter.

"Each of these nectar flows has a unique flavor because of the flower it comes from," Drew tells me. While the orange blossom and palmetto are mono-floral sources (a single type of flower), the

spring and late-summer wildflowers mean the bees are pollinating multiple types of flowers that will impact the flavor of the honey. "In August and September, you'll have a lot of palm blooming, you'll have cabbage [palm], you'll have Brazilian pepper."

Drew is passionate about producing natural, single-origin honey. Big honey operations, he says, may not move their bees around; instead, they'll feed them genetically modified corn syrup year-round — which isn't great for the bees (or the humans consuming the honey) and does nothing to help pollinate our native plants and trees.

"If we bottle the honey as single origin from one farm, then we allow the honey to be nuanced by the season," Drew says. "And I believe that's the healthiest honey you can get."

Both Chef Ben and Drew stress the importance of eating local-to-you, naturally grown foods. It's a healthy option that supports the communities where we live (or as is the case for many of us, the Orlando community we regularly visit). Whether it's a meal at Maria & Enzo's or Space 220, a day trip off property to Southern Hill Farms (another Clermont farm and Chef Ben recommendation) for pumpkin picking and live music, or a quick drive to an Orlando farmers market (Sugar Top Farms is a regular at the Winter Park Farmers' Market) to stock your hotel room with fresh fruit all week, it's totally possible to support Central Florida farmers while also enjoying the magic of Disney.

DID YOU KNOW ?

Autumn at Disney Parks Around the World

BY HEATHER ADAMS

1 While Mickey's Not-So-Scary Halloween Party is *the* event of the season at Walt Disney World, it's a recent addition. The party first premiered at Magic Kingdom in 1995, and only after Disney World tried a number of other spooky events, including Halloween Weekend, which started in 1972 and lasted only two days. Since 1995, MNSSHP has grown increasingly bigger and ultimately morphed into today's family-friendly party.

2 In the 1970s, before Mickey's Not-So-Scary Halloween Party took off with guests, Disney World also tried out another frightfully fun party: the Village Halloween Party. Held at the Lake Buena Vista Shopping Village, this festive event welcomed both locals and guests of the resort to trick-or-treat through the stores. It didn't really take off, but the trick-or-treating aspect hung around — and today, the shopping center offers fall entertainment in its newest form as Disney Springs.

3 While guests of all ages can only dress up in costumes in Magic Kingdom for Mickey's Not-So-Scary, Tokyo Disney Resort actually welcomes costumes all throughout the Halloween season. Guests who visit Tokyo Disneyland and Tokyo DisneySea may visit in costume — regardless of age — every day while Disney Halloween is underway in September and October.

4 At Disneyland in Anaheim, Halloween — and other holiday celebrations — really didn't become popular until the mid-1990s. The park didn't officially host a seasonal event until 1995 (the same year as the first Mickey's Not-So-Scary Halloween Party at Magic Kingdom) when Mickey's Halloween Treat debuted.

5 Despite introducing a Halloween party of its own, Disneyland never really stuck with a set tradition — at least not until 2005, when Mickey's Halloween Treat returned to the resort at Disney California Adventure. Even so, the party's name changed multiple times (and it bounced back and forth across the Esplanade) until 2019, when the resort finally settled on an all-new event, title, and host park: Oogie Boogie Bash at California Adventure.

6 Now five years into its run, Disneyland Resort's Oogie Boogie Bash is hugely popular among locals. It's much more frightening than Magic Kingdom's Halloween festivities, featuring more villains and spooky special offerings such as Villains Grove. The biggest difference, though, is guests are *hugely* into costumes. If you don't don an over-the-top Disney-inspired costume for the party, you'll be an outlier.

7 Halloween might not be as big a deal culturally in China as it is in the U.S., but Shanghai Disney Resort certainly doesn't skip out on the celebration. One of the most exciting additions to the park during October? The Disney Villains who appear. From special themed photos featuring the villains to the Halloween Villains Fireworks Show, you can see plenty of characters who might not pop up often in the U.S. parks., including Captain Hook and the Queen of Hearts.

8 At Hong Kong Disneyland, Disney Villains take center stage during the month of October. While Halloween isn't a big cultural event here, the Hong Kong park offers a special event similar to Mickey's Not-So-Scary Halloween Party. Called Disney Halloween Time, this separately ticketed event focuses on how Disney Villains have restyled Hong Kong Disneyland into a fashion destination — and the night includes wicked surprises plus trick-or-treating at candy stations and after-hours park access.

9 If you're more into making mischief during Halloween than getting spooked, Disneyland Paris offers both a touch of frightening villains (who take over Sleeping Beauty Castle each night during the season) and plenty of lighthearted fun. During the park's annual Disney Halloween Festival, guests can celebrate with the Mischief Makers, a cast of Disney characters such as Daisy Duck, Chip 'n' Dale, and Goofy, who pull pranks and bring the laughs, all while dressed in their Halloween costumes.

Oogie Boogie is the star of the show at Disney California Adventure's Oogie Boogie Bash. **PHOTO BY JAYSEN WHITE**

WDW

MAGAZINE

CEO
Stephanie Shuster

CREATIVE DIRECTOR
Danny Shuster

COMMUNICATIONS DIRECTOR
Tatjana Lazar

MARKETING DIRECTOR
Christopher Flaherty

EDITORIAL DIRECTOR
Timothy Moore

GRAPHIC DESIGNER
Abby Richardson

STAFF
Heather Adams, Morgan Flaherty,
Jessica Huff, Jodi Spasovski,
Gregg Taylor

COPY EDITOR
Cathy Salustri

CONTRIBUTORS
Tina Chiu
Trisha Daab
Johnaé de Felicis
Brydie Huffman
Matthew Krul
Josie Maida
Brian McCumsey
Brooke McDonald
Stephen Stout

PHOTOGRAPHERS

Marisa Alvarado	Kenneth Palm
CJ Ayd	David Quintanilla
Nick Barese	Rich Ramos
Mike Billick	Laurie Sapp
Ernie Carr	Dom Tabon
Jeff Chiu	Cliff Wang
Judd Helms	Jaysen White
Andy Jerzewski	

SPECIAL THANKS
To Disney, for providing photos used
in this issue and for inviting us to the
opening of World Celebration and
to D23 2024: The Ultimate Disney Fan
Event; to Patina Restaurant Group, for
arranging an interview and providing
photos used in this issue; and to
Petal Honey, for participating in an
interview and providing photos used
in this issue.

MEMBERSHIP BENEFITS

Ready to take your membership to the next level? As a *WDW Magazine*
subscriber, you get FREE access to the Membership Center, home to
plenty of bonus perks such as:

 Access to exclusive Walt Disney World
area discounts

 Latest breaking Disney Parks news

 Current Disney travel special
promos and discount
listings

AND MORE!

Log in to the Membership Center and explore these bonus benefits!

NEXT MONTH

Can you go the distance? Our
November 2024 issue is all
about competition, from the silly
challenges you can tackle at the
parks (have you heard of the
World Showcase Carbo Load?) to
the fun sporting options Disney
World offers, such as FootGolf.
In this issue, we'll try to eat the
entire Kitchen Sink at Beaches
& Cream, learn all the secret
cheats on Toy Story Mania,
visit All-Star Sports Resort, and
learn how Walt's love of skiing
gave us the Country Bears.